The Beginner's Guide to Buying a Home

A Guide-Workbook that Takes You from Concept to Homeownership

R. Ceci Dymally
Realtor
DRE # 01417242

Publisher
Alfred Aaron Publishing
P.O.Box 361333
Los Angeles, CA 90036

Book Cover Design by Phillips Media

Interior Design by Jessica Tilles/TWA Solutions.com

ISBN# 978-0-692-12257-0

Legal Disclaimer:
This book is intended as a general guide to the topics discussed and not intended to deliver legal advice. It is not intended, and should not be used as a substitute for professional advice (legal or otherwise). You should consult a professional with specific issues or questions that you may have concerning your transaction.

This publication is designed to provide accurate and authoritative information in regard to the subject matter covered. It is sold with the understanding that the reader will consult a professional to facilitate their particular Real Estate transaction. If legal services or advice or other expert assistance is needed, the services of a competent professional should be sought.

By reading this book, you assume all risks associated with using the advice given herein, with a full understanding that you, solely are responsible for anything that may occur as a result of putting this information into caution in any way, regardless of your interpretation of the advice.

You further agree that the author, publisher cannot be held responsible in any way for the success or failure of your endeavors as a result of the information presented in this book. It is your responsibility to conduct your own due diligence if you intend to apply any of the information contained in the guide/workbook in any way.

This book is dedicated to my brother, Al Dymally

Thank you Brother dear for being my safety net! You are my inspiration in life. I watch you navigate through your life giving, helping, and being a man of honor and integrity.

You are an amazing Father, a cherished friend, a doer and a giver in society and the best, most loving brother a girl could have!

You inspire me every day to be a better human being! I thank you for loving me without judgment, for helping me without pause and for supporting with an enthusiastic unwavering encouragement. You are my rock in this world and I adore you!

Love always your big Sister!

FOR
SALE

CONTENTS

TO THE READER vii

SO YOU DECIDED TO BUY A HOUSE ix

1: KNOW THE BUYING PROCESS 1

ABC's - A Step by Step look at buying a house 1

Checklist 12

2: BEFORE BUYING A HOUSE 13

33 Key Questions to ask b4 buying a home 13

21 Essential Points you should do before buying a home 19

20 Important Tips for buying a home 22

Checklist 27

3: THINGS TO LOOK FOR WHEN BUYING A HOUSE 30

10 Things to watch for when buying a house 30

18 Open house Red flags 32

12 House Hunting Tips to help make the choice 35

6 Things I wish I knew when I bought my house 37

10 Things you need to know about buying a house 38

20 Things to consider beyond the inspection 40

Checklist 43

4: REAL ESTATE TIPS 48

24 Real Estate Tips 48

123's of Real Estate 51

ABC's of Buying a Short Sale Home 56

21 Real Estate Terms Every Home Buyer Should Understand 58

Checklist 62

5: THINGS TO DO AFTER YOU BOUGHT YOUR HOUSE 65

New home owner checklist—12 things to do right away 65

19 Ways immediately to save money 69

123's of moving in 74

Checklist 84

6: TASKS OF YOUR REALTOR—What do they really do? 87

WORKBOOK 95

Step 1: Deciding What You Want 97
Step 2: Choose a Lender 103
Step 3: Choose a Realtor 105
Step 4: Locate Your Property 107
Step 5: Make an Offer on the Property 109
Step 6: Within 3—7 Days After Acceptance of Offer 111
Step 7: Within 7—17 Days 112
Step 8: Verify Property with Lender 114
Step 9: Verification of Property Condition 116
Step 10: Signing Loan Documents 117
Step 11: What Are Closing Costs? 118
Step 12: Funding 119
Step 13: Recording 120
Step 14: Moving 121

JOURNAL 135

TO THE READER

Congratulations! You have just made one of the biggest decisions in your life—buying your first piece of property, upgrading or acquiring a secondary property.

It is my desire with this guide-workbook to remove the fear and uncertainty of the process of acquiring property. You may harbor tremendous apprehension as to what does the process entail? On one hand you are excited about buying a home or rental property but on the other hand you may be scared to death as to what you are getting yourself into!

"What am I going to have to go through? What will I need? Who do I call first? What do I do first? What will I be asked to do? How long does the process take?"

On and on and on...

The Beginner's Guide to Buying a Home was created by **R. Ceci Dymally, *Realtor*** with those very issues in mind. *"99% of my clients had the very same fears and concerns".*

So after many Real Estate transactions and discovering that each of my clients had the same questions time after time I put together this guide-workbook that will take you **from concept to homeownership!**

This guide/workbook was designed in an easy to follow format so that you can use it on your own or with the help of your Realtor. As you go through it, make sure you complete each section thoroughly.

My aim is to help as many people as possible acquire the American Dream of owning property while eradicating the fear through education and information.

God Bless you in your journey to acquire the American Dream with a smile on your face—without the stress!

R. Ceci Dymally
REALTOR
DRE # 01417242

So, You Decided to Buy a House

So you decided to buy a house! Now what? You are probably asking yourself," Where do I start? Who do I talk to first?" If you are like most 1st time home buyers - you have a lot of questions going on in your head that you need answers to. Whether this is your 1st purchase or not, buying a house can be very stressful. This guide/workbook will help you take some of the fear and uncertainty out of the process. You are not alone. The useful information contained in this guide along with the workbook should make the task so much easier and less overwhelming.

Before getting started on the journey - answer the questions below to give you a foundation of the essential information needed to secure the perfect property for you and your family.

Decide that you want to buy? Make sure that you are buying for the right reasons. Don't buy because of pressure from your peers, family or friends. Know your reasons for buying and make sure that they are sound and substantiated.

1. Why do you want to buy now? ______________________________

   ____

2. What is your motivation? ______________________________

   ____

3. What monthly amount can you comfortably afford? ________________
4. When do you want to move? Time frame? ____________________
5. How will you get the money to buy? Savings? Family etc. ______________

   ____

6. How much money do you have total for the purchase? ______________
7. Where do you want to move to? What area? ____________________

   ____

8. Who will you move in with? ____________________

____

9. Will you be buying this house on your own or with someone? ____________________

DECIDE THE HOUSE YOU WANT:

10. What are the basics? ____________________

____

____

____

____

11. Size - How big? ____________________

12. Are there a lot of windows? ____________________

13. Is it on a cul da sac; private community etc. ____________________

14. In the heart of the city, suburbs etc. ____________________

15. Does it have trees ____________________

16. Big backyard ____________________

17. Big Bedroom - den - office—garage ____________________

____

____

18. Etc. ____________________

____

____

____

____

____

Next - What does your dream house look like? Draw it out. It is essential to visualize exactly what you want.

Draw it out or place a picture - Map it out in detail

Gather Your Tribe—Your Support Team

You need to start compiling your support team. Purchasing a house is a team effort. It is not a task to be done alone. Start to ask friends and family for referrals to build your support team. Don't do this alone! Gather your Tribe.

Who is in your Tribe:

1. Lenders
2. Bankers
3. Real Estate Agents
4. Attorney
5. Escrow Companies
6. Inspection Company
7. Appraisers
8. Friends who have bought a house before

When you have decided who will be on your team, put together your list of your Tribe.

My Support Team

Lender: ______________________________

____

____

Real Estate Agent: ______________________________

____

____

Banker: ______________________________

____

____

Attorney: ______________________________

____

____

Appraiser: ______________________________

____

____

Inspector: ______________________________

____

____

Escrow: ______________________________

____

____

Insurance: ______________________________

____

____

Parent(s): ______________________________

____

____

Friend(s): ______________________________

____

____

Other(s): ______________________________

____

Decide your maximum budget to buy your house. What is the total cost of monies you will allocate to purchasing your home? There are some fees that must be paid up front. Other fees can be rolled into your home loan. It is important to understand the difference and know what you will be expected to pay out of pocket when you sit down at the closing table. Your budget should include but not exclusive to the following:

- Down payment
- Private mortgage insurance
- Homeowners Insurance
- Title Insurance
- Appraisal
- New Furniture
- Movers
- Redecoration
- Home inspection
- Lender fees
- Escrow fees
- Interest
- Taxes
- Repairs & Maintenance

Maximum Budgeted Amount $________________

Ready! Set! Go!

...but before you do:

- Know your credit score
- Call a lender and get qualified
- Get a Realtor

Then start looking with the map of your dream house in hand with the specifics.

Be patient during the process and never settle for less than what you want!

Pre-Purchase Summary Checklist

__________ Determine the specifics of your dream house

__________ Determine your maximum Amount Budgeted

__________ Find out your Credit score

__________ Call a lender and get qualified

__________ Get a Realtor

__________ Get Referrals' to build your Tribe

KNOW THE BUYING PROCESS

CHAPTER 1

In this chapter:

ABCs—A Step-by-Step Look at Buying a House

Buying Process Summary Checklist

ABC'S - A Step-by-Step Look at Buying a House

The way you navigate through the home buying transaction depends on the real estate laws and customs where you live, but there are certain steps to buying a house that are standard, even though they might not be accomplished in the same order in every location.

You will feel more confident about your home buying journey once you understand what is expected of you and others involved in the transaction.

These steps will take you through it, and show you the key steps to buying a house.

Every state requires slightly different steps to buying a home, although they are somewhat very similar. Here are the steps towards home ownership in California, broken down into simple steps:

A. Get Prequalified/Preapproved

- ► Order a free credit report online and fix any mistakes. Get started early with this process because if you have to fix an error, it could delay your ability to buy a house.
- ► Get a referral to a mortgage broker, but also compare rates offered by your own bank and/or credit union. Rates are not the sole reason to choose a lender because they change daily and hourly. Choose a lender who can perform and close on time.
- ► Ask the lender to give you a loan preapproval letter, which means the lender will verify your income and pull a credit report. This carries a lot more weight when you write an offer.

- Determine your maximum loan amount, but choose only a mortgage type that you understand and a payment level with which you feel comfortable, which may be less than the maximum for which you are approved.

B. Hire a Buyer's Agent

- A buyer's agent will represent only you and they have a fiduciary responsibility to look out for your best interests. *(A fiduciary is a person who holds a legal or ethical relationship of trust with one or more other parties. Typically, a fiduciary prudently takes care of money or other assets for another person)*. It is ideal to be represented by an agent whose sole practice is buyer representation. You do not have to work with an agent who also works with sellers, unless you want to.
- Buyer's agents may ask you to sign a buyer's broker agreement, but it is the seller who pays the commission.
- Interview agents until you find an agent that you can trust and with whom you feel comfortable. Possessing a real estate license is no guarantee your agent is competent so make sure that you take the time to determine their qualifications.
- Once you have settled on an area, try to hire a neighborhood specialist. An agent who routinely sells homes in the area where you want to buy will have more knowledge that could help guide your decision to buy.

C. Look at Homes for Sale

- Ask your agent to look at homes for you before showing them to you. Not every agent will have the time for this extra service, but in some instances, agents will agree.
- Narrow your search to those homes that fit your exact parameters to find that perfect home. This might be more difficult to accomplish in a market with tight inventory.
- Ask your agent to give you MLS print-outs of comparable sales in your targeted neighborhood. With printouts in front of you, you can take notes as you tour.
- Consider all homes on the market, including fixer-uppers, REOs, foreclosures, short sales and those overpriced homes with longer days on the market. You will find this approach helpful when your choices are slim.

- Observe open house etiquette. If you go to an open house without your Real Estate Agent, tell the hosting agent that you are represented by a real estate agent. (give them your Agent's business card)

- Tell your agent which online home listings you are interested in previewing and ask for additional input. Your agent can gather more information than the notes in the MLS by talking to the listing agent, and will get more insight than you could on your own, so don't call the listing agent yourself. Let your agent earn his or her paycheck and do this for you.

D. Write a Purchase Offer

- Consider writing seller's market offers in seller's markets and buyer's market offers in buyer's markets. The importance of this cannot be stressed enough. A "lowball strategy" does not work in seller's markets.

- Select a home offer price based on the amount you feel a seller will accept or counter. This price is generally based on the comparable sales, with input from your real estate agent.

- If you are considering a low-ball offer, ask your agent to substantiate this price for you. You will need to present a reason for the seller to accept this type of offer, and it should be based on a sensible strategy.

- Prepare for multiple offers if the home is considered desirable in a hot location. Don't be afraid of multiple offers. Somebody's offer has to be accepted. Why can't that buyer be you?

- If your offer is rejected, ask your agent to explain why and don't repeat that mistake with your next offer. Also, don't automatically blame your agent. Maybe the problem is you didn't offer enough?

E. Negotiate and Write Counter Offers

- Expect the seller to issue a counter offer. Even if you offered full list price, the seller might have other points that were not adequately addressed to the seller's satisfaction in the offer.

- If the seller counters at full price, continue to negotiate. Even if you offered less initially, you might find that continued negotiations could result in the final offering price that is acceptable to both of you. The first counter is not always the last.

- During offer negotiation, write a letter and share personal information about your family to give the seller a reason to care about you. Especially if there are other offers, you will want to put your best foot forward and have your offer resonate with the seller on a personal level.

F. Make an Earnest Money Deposit

- When your offer is accepted, deposit your earnest money check with the appropriate party. In California, it is 3 days to make the deposit.
- Do not ever make your check payable to the seller. Do not pay the seller directly.
- Your offer should contain contingencies that will return your earnest money deposit to you if you cancel the contract. Usually, the contingency periods will have a time period for performance.

G. Open Escrow/Order Title

- Your agent or transaction coordinator will open escrow and title, if the listing agent hasn't already done so.
- Ask for the escrow officer's name, phone, email, and escrow file number. Escrow officers are bound by confidentiality.
- Give this information to your lender and your insurance agent. Get an early start on obtaining quotes for an insurance policy as some insurance companies are reluctant to insure all homes in all neighborhoods.

H. Order Appraisal

- Your lender will require an advance payment for the appraisal. Every so often, a lender will as a promotion agree to pay for your appraisal. Ask about it.
- If you receive a low appraisal, discuss options with your agent. As a buyer, it is natural for you to want the seller to reduce the price, but that might not be the only solution. Get the facts.
- Ask for a copy of the appraisal. If you paid for the appraisal, you are entitled to receive it.

I. Comply With Lender Requirements

- Lenders may ask for additional information. Do not complain. They don't write all of the rules. It could be the difference between getting the loan and not getting the loan.
- Do not make home buying mistakes such as altering your financial situation while in escrow. Please do not make any major purchases or acquire any additional debt. It can stop you from buying a house.

- When the file is complete, the lender will submit it for final underwriter approval.

J. Approve Seller Disclosures

- Read and question items you do not understand on the TDS (Transfer Disclosure Statement), Seller Property Questionnaire, natural hazard report, pest inspection/completion and other documents such as a preliminary title policy.
- Realize you have 10 days to review for lead-based paint, which is a federal disclosure.
- Read every document in its entirety; ask questions about all seller disclosures. If you encounter unfamiliar terminology, ask your agent to explain it to you.

K. Order Homeowner's Insurance Policy

- Order your homeowner's insurance early. As mentioned earlier, not every insurance company will insure every home, especially older homes or homes located in hazardous places.
- Sometimes previous claims by a homeowner can make it difficult to get insurance. A C.L.U.E. report will disclose previous claims.
- Get replacement coverage. It doesn't cost that much more to obtain replacement coverage, which will rebuild your home if it is destroyed. Sadly, many victims of wildfires did not carry replacement coverage.

L. Conduct Home Inspection

- Hire a reputable home inspector. Not every state requires inspectors to be licensed.
- Bring a home inspection checklist with you. You will want to make sure every area of concern has been inspected and your questions addressed.
- Attend the home inspection. Do not follow the home inspector around. Let the inspector do the job of inspection in peace. Wait until the home inspector is finished before asking questions.

M. Issue Request for Repair

- If the home inspection turns up significant and unexpected problems, issue a request for repair by asking the seller to address those issues, give you a credit toward closing costs or lower the sales price. Realize the seller might say no.

- Realize no home is perfect, and the inspector will find faults. Don't expect everything on the home inspection report to be fixed.
- Be reasonable by making rational inquiries. Your agent can guide you.

N. Remove Contingencies

- For example by default, California C.A.R. contracts give you 17 days to remove contingencies. The contingencies do not expire at the end of 17 days.
- Try to make sure your loan is firm and the appraisal is acceptable before removing your loan contingency. If your lender can't confirm your loan, you might still need to remove the loan contingency, if you are contractually obligated to.
- If you do not remove contingencies, the seller can issue a Notice to Perform and then unilaterally cancel the contract.

O. Do Final Walk-Through

- Do not pass up doing a final walk-through. You might be tempted to forgo this formality, but those who choose that option often regret that decision.
- Inspect the property to make sure it's in the same condition as when you agreed to buy it. This is not a license to demand more repairs unless you find a new defect not previously disclosed.
- If you find a serious issue, address it now before you close. Due to the urgency of some situations, you might find a fast solution that will not hold up closing. Try to avoid financial arrangements that could change your closing disclosure or your loan docs could need to be redrawn.

P. Sign Loan/Escrow Documents

- For example, in southern California, you will sign escrow documents shortly after opening escrow. During escrow, you will receive other documents.
- In northern California, you will sign escrow documents along with your loan documents near closing. You will generally sign a few days prior to actual recordation.
- Bring a valid picture ID. Make sure the name on your ID is the same name as on your loan documents.

Q. Deposit Funds

- Bring a certified check payable to escrow. You cannot deposit cash or a personal check. Personal checks are acceptable if there is adequate time to clear prior to closing.
- Expect escrow to pad the amount, so you may receive a refund after closing. Escrow can mail you the check or wire the refund to your bank.
- Consider asking your bank to wire the funds directly to escrow, saving you the hassle of physically delivering the cashier's check to escrow.

R. Close Escrow

- Your property deed, seller's reconveyance and deed of trust will record in the public records. Later, weeks after closing, you will receive the original deed in the mail.
- The title company will notify your agent when your transaction records, and in turn, it is common for your agent to call you. Many Real Estate Agents are very excited when it's time to hand over keys to your new home to you.
- After recordation, unless your contract specifies otherwise, the property is yours — change the locks immediately.

S. After Closing

- The closer at the closing should have given you a packet with copies of all of the closing docs and mortgage papers in it. Make sure you find a safe place to sort those documents. You should receive a copy of the deed from the County in about a month. Put that with your closing packet.
- For most closings you would now be pretty much home free.

T. Issues & after closing potential dangers

- If you were provided with a Home Warranty as part of the deal, it's a good idea to call the company and just make sure that they have your contact information correctly recorded in their database. Also put the warranty brochure or other paperwork that you received somewhere safe and somewhere that you can remember if you need to call in a problem. Remember that all of the warranty companies require that you call them first, so that they can dispatch someone from their list of contract repair people. If you call your own plumber first, they will not reimburse you.

- Make sure to contact the various utilities to check that they have done any final readings that were requested and transitioned the accounts into your name.

- If you are on city water and sewer you may have to wait until the next billing cycle before the bill can be pro-rated between you and the seller. Check with the city water department on how they will do that. If the bill comes to the house, contact the title company that represented the seller and get them a copy of the bill. They are responsible for paying the pro-rated portion that the seller owes. You may have to send it through your agent and the listing agent to get it to the right place.

- You should have the door locks re-keyed. Even if the seller gave you all of the keys that they had to the place there could be others out there in the hands of relatives or neighbors. It's just good practice to change the locks when you change ownership.

- What about if you find something unexpected wrong with the house now? Well, at this point it's your house. You had your chances at the inspections and final walk-through to uncover those things. It is possible that the old owner was unaware of the problem, so don't immediately assume that this was some defect that they hid from you. Hopefully it is covered under the home warranty. If not, it is your problem now as the new owners.

- If it is an issue concerning a cloud on the title (a long lost relative suddenly showing up and claiming a right to the property) call the title company. It is their responsibility to protect you against that type of claim.

- It can get a little hairy if it involves an unrecorded lien (or tax) against the property. You can make the case that the title company should have found that lien and they will fight back that it was not recorded anywhere and their title clearly states that they are insuring you against recorded issues. If it turns out to be a tax issue the title company probably should have caught that and you should challenge your case with them.

- It is possible that the old owners did hide some material facts from you; things like the fact that they finished the basement themselves without pulling permits (lots of homeowners do that) or that the deck that they built out back actually encroaches 5 feet into the rear neighbor's yard. Those "facts" should have been disclosed on the Seller's Disclosure, so maybe you think that was a fraudulent document; however, we have just stepped across the line from real estate into legal matters, so it is advised that you find a good lawyer to handle your questions on what to do about that.

U. Smooth Transition

Here are some additional things you should do to make sure your transition from your old place to your new address go as smoothly as possible.

Every area of the country is different, which can mean different protocols and rules to follow. But no matter where you live, here are a few important things to do after you get possession of your house.

- Hire a Pest Control Company—If you are in an area with warm climates, they may have lots of ants, cockroaches and other bugs.
- Change Your Driver's License—Every state is different, but some states require a change of address on your license within 10 days of moving. If you are new to a state, you may have to take a written exam and possibly even a driving test.
- Secure Closing Papers and Other Documents—If you haven't done so already, get a safe deposit box at your bank or purchase a fireproof safe. Put all your closing papers inside it, along with your passport, birth certificate, Social Security card and other official papers for safe keeping.
- Check with Your Auto Insurance—Insurance companies are picky about where you live, and prices do change from place to place.
- Contact Government Officials about Homesteading—You can get a reduction in your assessed value by thousands of dollars—which gives you a discount on your property taxes—by just filling out a form saying you occupy the home you just bought. Some counties give other homestead exemptions like for senior citizens or returning veterans. This doesn't happen automatically. You have to tell them you live there. It all depends on your city or your county of what type of homestead credit is available.
- Clean the Gutter—Who knows how long it's been since the previous owners cleaned the gutters. But if leaves and other gunk are blocking the flow of rain, you could have problems such as water leaking into the house if you don't keep them free flowing.
- Meet Your Neighbors and Others in the Community—Get to know your neighbors by introducing yourself.
- Hire A Fireplace Expert—If you have a fireplace, whether it's a wood burning or gas fireplace, get a professional to check it out. With thumbs up from the expert, you can then enjoy cozy nights near the warmth of the fire.

- Change Furnace Filters—It's best if you make sure to replace furnace and air conditioner filters every three months. There are lots of options out there when choosing air filters for different seasons. Choosing the right filter can not only save money by letting your furnace and air conditioner work more efficiently, but it also improves air quality, removes odors and even prevents growth of antimicrobial particulates.

- Find The Main Water Shutoff—You never know when you will need to shut off the water because of a broken water pipe. So, find the shutoff and test it to see if it works.

- Change Every Lock—You never know who the former owners gave a house key to. A locksmith can rekey your locks if they are expensive ones, and some stores can also rekey certain brand named locks, which can be done quite inexpensively. You can also choose to get four digit keyless locks. That can be a great option especially with kids who lose their keys all the time anyways. Also, don't forget to reset a garage door keypad from the outside of your garage.

- Cover The Windows—The former owners might have taken all the curtains and blinds with them. So before your neighbors get to know you real well because they can see through your windows, purchase coverings to give yourself some privacy.

V. Moving in

- DON'T move everything yourself—Hire MOVERS if at all possible.
- Take the pressure off yourself—Do NOT try to complete the entire move in 4 hours.
- Pack everything that you care about . . . ONLY the stuff that matters to you . . and move ONLY that—Garage sale, donate, and gift the rest. Downsize!
- Set the technology up FIRST. Begin with the stereo, IPod, Echo and docking speaker and crank up your favorite music—This is ESSENTIAL—Do this before placing the first piece of furniture or unpacking the first box.
- Move ALL of the little stuff (Boxes) into the garage or one large room and forget about it until later—The only exception being the Kitchen boxes
- Then, set up your entertainment system
- Then, set up your computer network

- There's nothing worse than trying to set those electronics up when you're tired and cranky, and the house is completely out of order being half unpacked.
- Next . . . Set up the BEDS . . . ALL of the beds—Nothing else. Set them up COMPLETELY—sheets and all—So they're ready for you when you fall down later.
- Next . . . Unpack the KITCHEN boxes and get that space set up enough to be functional . . . Once the kitchen is set up, enjoy a beverage, cook a nice dinner and relax for a little while in your new house.
- If you don't feel like doing anything else after dinner, resist because the beds are ready, use them! Relax and don't overdo do it!
- When you're ready to continue the settling in, place all of the large furniture
- Now—over time—take one box at a time out of the garage and unpack each one completely before getting the next one. This "Exercise" of unpacking boxes could easily take some time to finish. You are not allowed to park your car in the garage until you are done
- Now, it's time to build a list of things you need and things you've discovered you want to change or fix in the house. Don't do ANY of these things yet, just build the list.
- After ALL of the boxes are unpacked, start on the list.
- Don't make this process high pressure or priority. Be kind to yourself and your family. Don't rush this. There will be plenty of time to manicure the lawn and personalize the house later so don't do all that until you're settled in.
- Send a thank you note to your REALTOR for guiding you through this process. The best way to thank your REALTOR, Loan Broker and all key players in the transaction is to give them referrals.
- And by all means, don't ever forget that your REALTOR will be your Real RESOURCE forever. Keep their information handy.

Buying Process Summary Checklist

_______ Get Prequalified/Preapproved

_______ Hire a Realtor

_______ Look at Homes

_______ Find a Home

_______ Write an offer—Negotiate & Write Counter Offers

_______ Make an Ernest Money Deposit

_______ Open Escrow/Order Title

_______ Order Appraisal

_______ Comply with Lender Requirements

_______ Approve Seller Disclosures

_______ Order Homeowners Insurance Policy

_______ Conduct Home Inspection

_______ Issue Request for Repair

_______ Remove Contingencies

_______ Do Final Walk Through

_______ Sign Loan/Escrow Documents

_______ Deposit Funds

_______ Close Escrow

_______ After Closing

_______ Issues & After closing Potential Dangers

_______ Smooth Transaction after care

_______ Move in

BEFORE BUYING A HOUSE

CHAPTER
2

In this chapter:

33 Key Questions to Ask Before Buying a House

21 Essential Things You Should Do Before Buying A House

20 Important Tips For A Buying A Home

Checklists

33 Key Questions to Ask Before Buying a House

1. Will the Windows need to be replaced?

   Did you know that new windows can cost $10,000 or more? How often do you walk into a house and inspect the windows? If anything, we enjoy the *shape* of them, the *position* of them, the scenery *outside* of them, but rarely do we consider the *condition* of the windows. Windows are costly and they're one of the most costly home repairs and upgrades that you'll ever pay for. This is not the kind of expense you want to pay when you move into a house. So get a house with solid windows that will keep you warm in the winter and cool in the summer.

2. What's the position and quality of the trees around the house?

   In a bad storm trees could fall on your new house. Do any of them look rotted? Do any of them need to be cut down? Do those trees block the sunrise? What about the sunset? Look to see if there are leaves on the trees. *Who* even notices bare trees in the winter? A tree that has a lot of leaves can be a problem when they fall.

3. Have there ever been any pest infestations?

   If there was an infestation, when were pest control procedures undertaken? No, this won't necessarily mean the house is pest-free at the time you're buying it, but it's a good starting point to know the history. Many buyers require that termite treatment be included in the price; it's easiest to tent for pest removal when the house is empty, between owners.

   Could you imagine buying a house and finding *roach infestation?* You need to be vigilant about pests when you're looking at houses. Look for mouse droppings. Ask the sellers for more information about it. Look inside cabinets and moist places where pests like to hide. Pull the refrigerator or stove out, and make sure there's nothing there! Check for ants, spiders etc

4. Does the neighborhood have sidewalks?

   Because you were excited about the house you didn't even notice that there are no sidewalks in the neighborhood. If you've got kids, or nieces and nephews that come to visit, get a house with some sidewalks. Even if you have no children, for your own safety when walking or jogging, buy a home in a neighborhood where there are sidewalks. Older homes and certain neighborhoods tend to have no sidewalks.

5. Is the house out dated?

   No house is going to be perfectly upgraded, especially if it's at a great price. Maybe love the beauty of the bay window, or the lovely wood floors. Sometimes a home's *potential* is its selling feature, along with the price and the promise of its beauty. But you must take a hard look at how outdated the house really is. How much will it cost to upgrade your new home? How much *time* will be involved if you attempt some DIY projects yourself? Are you being realistic regarding what you can accomplish, in time and budget? If you have kids, consider if you'll have enough time away from the kids to get these projects done. Otherwise, you may end up years later with rooms still with the ugly wallpaper because there just isn't enough time to change it.

6. Does the house have any funny odors?

   What do you smell when you walk into the house? If you smell a strong pungent smell that can be a bad sign! Pay attention. Because, seriously, if the house smells bad, it could be mold or mildew, dirty people, or cooking smells that hang in the air due to poor ventilation. Don't just think that you can "air a home out" after settlement. When you walk into a house you'd like to buy, it should not have a pungent smell. There shouldn't be any odors that try to make the house smell good either because that could be hiding something. You should smell very little. Homes that leave an odor means that you will be dealing with the odor when you move in, or it may be covering up other smells you don't even realize are there until you move in. Sometimes this can be a costly problem to clear up, depending on its cause. Check the smells.

7. Does the ground seem to slope away from the house?

   Does the house sit at the top or bottom of a hill? Where does the water flow around the house? Grading is probably one of the few things people check when they go house-hunting. Don't make this mistake! Grading that is poor and allows rain and water to sit at the home's foundation is a recipe for flooding and water damage. Grading isn't cheap to fix. Expect to pay upwards of $2,500 to have a professional landscaper or grading professional to re-grade the entire perimeter of your home.

8. What do the cars in the neighborhood look like?

   Take a look around you. If you see broken-down cars, expect to find a broken-down neighborhood. The cars don't have to be BMWs and Audis. But look for late model cars that look well-cared for. The quality of the cars, really can tell you a lot about the quality of a neighborhood.

9. What are the neighbors like?

   Go up and knock on the doors of the nearby neighbors and tell them you're planning to make an offer on the house next door or across the street. See what they say. Are they nice? Are they gossiping about the other neighbors that are moving out? What does their yard look like? Be sure to talk to *all* the neighbors. Do they have something negative to say about certain neighbors? Choose your neighbors wisely because you don't want to end up not liking your neighbors.

10. How much are the utilities for the house?

    Your usage will be different, depending on your family size but make sure that you inquire about the utility costs. Calling ahead to the utility companies will give you a great starting point to use when creating your budget, to make sure you can afford the property *and* all the things that go into moving into a new or larger home. There are tons of expenses you don't even realize up front that you'll need to pay when you move into a new house, but if you can nail down the utilities ahead of time you will not put yourself in a bad financial situation.

11. Are there any sex offenders in the neighborhood?

    The last thing you want is to buy a house next to a registered sex offender two doors down. Checking for sex offenders in the area isn't something most people do before buying a house, but it should be one of the first things you do especially if you have children. Be sure you know where they live, and be cautious of buying a house near them. Search for sex offenders at Criminal Watch Dog and Family Watch Dog.

12. Is there radon gas in the house?

    Radon is a colorless, odorless, radioactive gas that's found in about 1 out of every 15 homes. Rock and other things break down in the ground and radon is naturally released. It's found in lower levels outdoors, but indoors, it can be much higher. Above safe levels, it can cause lung cancer.

13. How do the schools rate in that area?

    Even if you don't have small kids, how the schools rank means a great deal. Because eventually you'll sell your house, and the next buyers may have kids. If the schools are horrible consider that in terms of resale value. The quality of schools affect home values. Check the school rankings on GreatSchools.org. Even if you have no children, it would be wise to buy in as good of a school district as possible.

14. Are the gutters in good condition?

    Check out the gutters! Gutters are expensive home repairs! Quotes to repair gutters can range as high as $5,000. Do any of them look bent? If it's raining, is water pouring over the gutters? Are there gutter guards in place? Do they work well? Ask the sellers how well the guards work at keeping out leaves and debris. Are the downspouts in good condition? Where do the downspouts empty out the water? Is the water emptying next to the house or away from the house?

15. How much noise do you hear in the neighborhood?

    The noise you hear during the day when people are at work may be different from the noise at night. Be sure to ride by the house during the day and night so you'll know. Also drive by weekdays and week*ends*. Is there a hospital nearby? Will an ambulance drive by at 2 a.m., blaring their sirens? Is there an airport nearby or loud jets landing at 10 p.m? What about trains nearby? Do they blow their horns? Is there a guy that lives next door and runs his power tools at all times of the day and night? You need to know this.

16. Have there been any new renovations on the home lately?

    Some have said that no one renovates their house to sell unless they're trying to hide something. Not every renovation has to be so sneaky, but you never know. Is there fresh paint in the basement, covering up water stains? Is there anything else that they've replaced just to sell? What's the real story behind their renovations? Ask about the renovation and why they decided to renovate at this point before the sale of the home. Sometimes a home looks brand-spanking new because it was recently renovated by investors that bought the property for a discount, fixed it up, and then re-listed it for a profit. If that's the case, then that would be fine. Just do your research and ask your real estate agent if that particular investor has a good reputation in the area for quality rehabs.

17. What would your commute to work be like?

    Imagine finding *the* perfect house and it's only 20 miles from your place of work! But little did you know that 20 miles takes 1.5 hours on a good day? Is that acceptable for you? If you've found a house you really like, wake up extra early and see if you can run that morning commute around the same time you would be if you were to buy the house. What about the evening commute? Instead of going home after work, drive to the prospective house and see if you can handle the commute. If you can't handle the commute, it's not the house for you, no matter how perfect it may seem.

18. How old are the appliances?

    This is something that a home inspector will tell you during an inspection, but decide to be proactive and look for this info while you're at the open house! If you knew that you were going to have to spend about $5,000 into new appliances or repairs, you may be able to adjust your offer price accordingly or you may decide not to even put an offer on the house. Don't wait until you've gotten so far into the process only to find out at the home inspection that the appliances are very old and will need to be replaced as soon as you move in. Know this information up front so that you can either walk away or be able to use that info to come up with a reasonable offer.

19. Are there bathroom vents?

Perform a spot-inspection of the heating and cooling units in the home. If you see rust, water marks or any other types of decay, or if you hear loud, strange noises, the systems may be too old.

20. What are the toilets like?

Check to see if there is a leak at the base of a toilet. The leak often appears small or insignificant, but over time the water will begin to rot the subfloor and even get between the subfloor and the finished floor. Someone unaware of the damage this kind of problem can create may try to seal these themselves, sometimes making it worse.

Here are some toilet leak signs to look for: First, look for discoloration and/or warping around the base of the toilet. Second, check if the floor moves or feels soft around the base of the toilet by applying body weight with your foot. Finally, the toilet bowl should not have any movement. It should feel solid, and when grasped on either side, should not rock or slide. If movement is noted it either has a bad seal, the flange is not secured, or the toilet is not secured to the flange.

21. What is the humidity level?

It's important to maintain the proper humidity levels in your home to keep a comfortable, healthy space. Indoor humidity levels should be between 30 to 50 percent, with the ideal level being about 45 percent.

22. Did the seller have pets?

When you are checking out a house you think you would like to buy - check the carpets with a black light to see if there is evidence of pet urine. Initially you may not notice any pet odors or even during inspection so make sure that at some point you get one of the black light flashlights and scan the floors and walls.

23. Are some parts of the house a different temperature than the rest?

One reason this may be is that the rooms nearest your furnace or cooling unit will get the most conditioned air. Rooms which sit further away, at the ends of the ducts, receive far less conditioned air. This may make them warmer than the areas at the heart of the house.

24. What's the neighborhood like at night?

Be sure to visit the neighborhood you're considering to move into at night as well as during the day. Some areas have a totally different feeling when the sun goes down; for instance, they might become a little shady, derelict or potentially dangerous.

25. How much are the property taxes?

    Property tax history is also typically available right on the listing detail page. If you can't find it, ask the seller. You'll want to find out what previous owners paid, but understand that the property tax, since it's based on a percentage of the value of the house, will probably be affected by your purchase price. This could be a huge additional expense, and you'll need to budget for that when putting together your offer.

26. What are the monthly maintenance and utility costs?

    Are there any type of homeowner's association fee? Find out. Also learn what kind of power the house uses, be it gas, oil, electric, or a combination, and ask what the average monthly bill for each is. Also inquire about water, waste removal, and any other utility costs that are applicable.

27. Has there ever been a broken pipe? Sewer backup?

    According to the Insurance Information Institute, broken pipes account for an estimated 22% of all home insurance losses. If the homeowner doesn't tell you, a good home inspector can probably find evidence of either one of these situations, so you might want to put these on your list of questions to ask your inspector, too.

28. How old is the roof?

    The National Association of Realtors® says the national median cost of an asphalt roofing replacement is about $7,600. It would be good to know how soon you might need to lay out that substantial amount of cash.

29. Are there warranties on the appliances, HVAC system, garage door, etc.?

    And if so, can the homeowner provide the documentation? Ask for it. This can establish how old these features are, and give you an idea of when they might need to be replaced and how expensive it could be. It will also help you decide whether or not to buy a home warranty.

30. What are the parking restrictions around the house?

    Will guests need parking permits? How many permits are you, as the homeowner, allowed, and can you obtain more if you decide to throw a party? Also, check out the parking situation on the property itself. Will your car(s) fit in the garage? Is there room to park anywhere else on the property other than the driveway?

31. Does the house have any kind of unusual history?

    In many states, owners are legally bound to disclose if a death or major crime has occurred recently on the premises, but there are other circumstances you should be aware of as well. For example: Did anyone famous ever live there? Was it ever used in a film, TV series, or commercial? If so, you might have to deal with fans ringing your doorbell or driving by at all hours of the day or night. Also ask if the house has a history of being haunted or paranormally stigmatized.

32. What is the crime rate in the neighborhood?

    It's important to be proactive about your safety, especially when it comes to choosing a place to live. After all, the safety of your neighborhood impacts everything from your happiness and sense of security to your home's resale value. Fortunately, there are several online tools that can help you check neighborhood crime rates.

33. How far is the nearby hospital or police station?

    Be sure to determine how far or close the nearby hospital or police station is.

    To find your neighborhood hospital - http://www.ushospitalfinder.com/

    To find your neighborhood police station - http://www.lapdonline.org/

21 Essential Things You Should Do Before Buying A House

1. Double Check the Facts

   Don't take the information contained in the listing as absolute truth. Be inquisitive and double check all of the facts. Most financial information contained on the actual MLS (Multiple Listing Service) listing is entered by the listing agent manually. This leaves room for error, so make sure the buyer's agent double checks these facts directly with the source, like HOA offices, county tax pages, etc.

2. Know the Value of the Home

   It is very important that a buyer work with an agent who is very familiar with pricing homes. A buyer's agent can cost a buyer hundreds of dollars in inspection costs and appraisal fees if they are not 100 percent familiar with the value of a home. Banks and sellers are not willing to reduce price on low appraisals like they have in recent years. Buyers need to be aware of this.

3. Interview Multiple Agents and Lenders

   Just as you may get multiple estimates for car repairs or second and third opinions from doctors, do your homework to ensure you get involved with the right lender and Real Estate agent from the beginning. You need to go with the agent and loan officer who are going to get it right the first time.

4. Consider All the Expenses

   Your new mortgage will be the biggest chunk of your new expenses when you close on a home. But it's far from the only one—and you've got to work all the numbers into a budget you can afford. Make sure that you have enough income and a budget, with money set aside not just for your monthly mortgage payments but also for insurance, association fees, possible repair work that may be needed as well as those unexpected expenses that are guaranteed to come up. And don't forget about property taxes!

5. Check for Outstanding Permits

   Make sure that you check for any outstanding permits on properties you may be considering. Most every house has had some renovations, and many renovations are done without permits. No permits mean no one inspected the work. You want to know if the property has been inspected.

6. Hire a Home Inspector

   Even if you feel you can trust the seller and your own inspection skills, hire a professional home inspector. It is a good idea if the inspector is a member of the American Society of Home Inspectors.

7. Check for Asbestos

   Any home built before 1980 might contain asbestos, so make sure you check for it to protect your family's safety. Get tiles, plaster and attic insulation tested especially if you plan on doing any renovations.

8. Check the Wiring

   Check for knob and tube wiring in any home you're considering. If a home was built before 1930, there's a good chance it still has knob and tube wiring. If it does it could affect your insurance policy. And bringing it up to code is an expensive job.

9. Check for Water Issues

   Look for potential water concerns, both inside and outside the home, which includes the roof, grading around your house, downspouts, moisture in your basement, trees near your roofline and tree roots around your foundation. They're all signs that could lead to bigger problems down the road. And better to know about them now—before they're officially your problem and expense.

10. Settle on a Price you are Comfortable with

    Just because you qualify for a loan doesn't mean that you'll be comfortable with the monthly mortgage. So figure out what best works for your budget. Before looking at houses, before meeting with a loan officer, take a look at your overall financial picture and determine a monthly payment that you are comfortable with.

11. Consider HOAs Carefully

    In community living situations like condominium buildings, you'll encounter "HOA"—homeowner association—fees. Make sure you factor these into your financial plans, and consider the prospect carefully. You have to understand everything included in that payment. You should know whether the association is financially healthy before you get involved. Many associations are struggling because of the foreclosures and poor economy. If the roof needs to be replaced, is there money available from the association to do so, or will you be assessed and have an additional, unexpected expense?

12. Review Your Credit Score

    Know your credit score before you set out on your search. You can borrow more money the higher your score is, and you'll pay less over the life of it, too, and to take advantage of the lowest possible rates, aim to have your score 700 or above. If you're credit score is not where you want to be, consider pausing the home search until you can work your score up a bit by paying all your bills on time and lowering your debt-to-credit limit ratio.

13. Get Pre-Approved for a Loan

    It is important to get a loan approval ahead of time. That way, when you walk into a home you love, you lower the risk of losing it to a buyer who looks more serious to the seller. Pre-approval puts you ahead of other buyers when it's time to negotiate and place an offer. And it helps you understand your limitations.

14. Find a Local Agent

    Locate and work with a real estate agent who is an expert in the precise neighborhoods that interests you. Those agents are most likely to know the comparables and help you jump on the right opportunity at the right price with no delay.

15. Avoid Change

    If you are looking to buy quickly, try to avoid any other major changes around the same time. A large change, like moving to a new job, could affect your mortgage approval, also even a small change, like changing banks, stands to slow down the process of verifying your checking and other monetary assets.

16. Don't Get Hung Up on Small Stuff

    When visiting potential homes to purchase, make sure that you look behind the furniture and decor of the existing owners because once they've moved out, you're left with the shell and your furniture. It's also very tempting to consider a home just as it is and decide whether or not you love it or hate it. But don't miss an opportunity just because you can't get past a small issue that can easily be changed to suit your tastes or needs—or even because you can't stand the way the seller's clutter looks in the house.

17. Envision a Fresh Coat of Paint

    Maybe that hot pink former kids' room or neon green bathroom doesn't appeal on first glance. But don't dwell on that. A fresh coat of paint can instantly enliven a space and transform it to your personal tastes affordably. Paint can truly change a space, so look beyond the existing wall colors, and instead focus on the layout and the space plan.

18. Consider Your Existing Furniture

    If you just bought a new house and unexpectedly have to buy all new furniture to go along with it, you could be blowing your budget right off the bat. So if you intend to move with your existing furniture, make sure you have a plan in place to make that feasible.

19. Focus on the Kitchen and Bathrooms

    The two most important spaces to focus on when buying a home are the kitchen and bathroom. Look at the condition and wear of the cabinetry, plumbing, appliances, hardware in the space. Some questions to ask yourself are: Are the spaces in good condition? Do I have a budget to renovate the space? If not, can I update the space with do-it-yourself projects?

20. Consider Your Investment Potential

    If you buy the largest, most expensive home in an area, know that there may be little potential for your investment to grow.

21. Be Patient—If You Can

    Short sales and foreclosures can lead to great deals if your situation allows you to wait out the bank delays.

20 Important Tips For Buying A Home

What are the most important things to do before buying a house? Being informed is important when you are making big financial decisions, and there are few financial decisions bigger than buying a home. Take the time to educate yourself about what you are getting into before you commit to buying any property. The following tips are here to help you get started. These 20 things to do before the purchase of a house will put you in a position for not only a smooth transaction but a pleasant first time home ownership experience.

1. Know your credit score.

   Your credit score is one of the biggest factors in what your loan terms will be. Know your score before you ever try to get a loan, and take the time to repair it if it is lower than 700. A good score which leads to a low-interest rate can save you tens of thousands of dollars over the life of the loan.

2. Have a lender pre-approve you before shopping.

   What to do before buying a house includes getting pre-approved. In fact, it is one of the most important parts of the home buying process! Pre-approval means you should be able to get the loan as long as nothing changes about your financial situation or your credit score.

   A pre-approval letter also helps when you want to compete with another buyer for a home you love. One of the first things most sellers are going to ask their agent when receiving an offer is how qualified the buyer is. Sellers want to feel comfortable knowing the buyer is not going to get turned down for the loan. A home buyer should understand there is a difference between a mortgage pre-approval and a pre-qualification. To get pre-approved lenders will verify employment, income, and credit. This is not the case with a pre-qualification.

3. Shop the lender.

   While getting pre-approved for a mortgage is a significant step for a first-time buyer so is shopping for the best deal. You will be paying the mortgage for a while so getting the lowest mortgage rate should be one of your prime considerations. Be sure to look at the annual percentage rate you are paying (commonly referred to as the APR) so you can compare. With some loans, you may be paying more points or have higher closing costs than others. So when you are shopping for the best mortgage, don't just look at the rate but the whole package.

4. Know every expense.

   There are a lot of fees that come with a home purchase above and beyond the mortgage. Insurance, repairs, association fees, property taxes—you should have the income and the budget to handle all of these things if they are relevant to your purchase. Real Estate agents can help you identify additional expenses to consider when buying a home. You should also have some savings to cover emergencies with the home.

5. Know what you want.

   Do you want a home or a condo? For many first time home buyers, this is one of the first dilemmas they will try to solve. In fact, many buyers will look at both because they can't make up their mind. To make sound decisions, you should know the pros and cons of a condo vs. a house. More buyers will end up disappointed when picking a condo because they did not understand the ramifications of how restrictive they can be or how quickly fees can change. The appeal, of course, is usually for those buyers who do not have time for home maintenance.

   After the excitement of buying the home passes, you will have to live in it for years. Make sure you are shopping for a home that will meet your needs and your lifestyle long term. More space is not always better. Lawns require upkeep. Being close to the things you like may wind up being more important than you realize. Understand you are not just buying a home but a location as well. One of the key considerations that many buyers miss when purchasing a home is knowing how to pick a neighborhood they will love. Often first time buyers focus too much on the house and not enough on the neighborhood.

6. Work with a skilled Realtor that knows your area.

   Every neighborhood has its unique qualities that you want to be aware of before you buy. An agent that is well-informed about the area will also know what homes in that area are worth, which will help you avoid overpaying for a property. You want a real estate agent who knows the area locally!

Make sure you interview several different buyers' real estate agents. Choose someone that is full time working in the business every day and has a recent history of successful sales. The better the real estate agent knows the area, the better equipped they will be in understanding the differences in market value from one property to the next.

7. Understand the actual value of any property you are buying.

   Working with a real estate agent that understands market values in your area is critical if you want to avoid overpaying for your house. In addition to the actual purchase price, there are other fees like appraisal and inspections that can cost you more when you don't understand the value of the home. Sellers and banks may not be flexible should you ask about adjusting the price later.

8. Buy what you are comfortable paying for.

   You may be cleared for a loan that is far above what you are comfortable paying for. Lean on the side of caution and mortgage only as much money as you are comfortable with. There are a lot of home buyers who will mortgage themselves to the max only to find out later they are a slave to their home.

9. Verify all information in the listing.

   You need to verify that all the information given about the home is right. Sometimes real estate agents put things in the listing that they may not have verified or may just not be aware of the facts. Some of the more common issues that can crop up in a real estate transaction is understanding what stays with a home and what doesn't. Many buyers, sellers, and even some real estate agents do not know what is considered a fixture and what personal property is.

10. Try to see yourself in the home.

    Sometimes when you view a home, it will be filled to the brim with the current owner's things. Learning to see past the clutter to the potential of the home may allow you to find better deals than you would otherwise. This is why real estate agents often recommend to seller clients to clear all the clutter before listing their home for sale. Cluttered homes can sell for less money when those with a lack of vision can't see past it.

11. Use a reputable home inspector.

    Find a home inspector that is a part of the American Society of Home Inspectors, or someone your real estate agent knows and trusts. You want someone who knows what they are doing and is not motivated to miss issues to encourage a sale. It is also advisable to find your inspector if you do not know your real estate agent well.

12. Make sure all renovations are up to code.

    If a renovation was done without a permit, it might not have been done right. No permit means that the work was not reviewed by an inspector, something you do not want in your new home. You might be wondering why a seller would bother not getting a permit for work done on their home. There are usually three reasons for this:

- By obtaining a permit for an addition, you will pay more money in taxes because your assessed value will go up with a larger home.
- It costs money to get permits. When you put on an addition, you are typically paying for permits for electrical, plumbing, and the general building inspector. Many owners just don't want to bother paying the fees.
- Pure laziness. This is what happens when some people don't want to take the time out of their day to get the permits required.

Buying a home without necessary building permits will become your issue in the future when you go to sell. It is advisable that you ask the seller to get the permits taken care of before you buy the home.

13. Make sure you understand the HOA that you will be part of.

Some homes are part of a homeowner association. All condominiums also have HOAs. These organizations are mandatory if you live in the area, so you will have to pay dues and rely on the association to take care of certain things, like maintenance of common areas. Some homeowners associations are great, some are not. Know what you are getting yourself into before purchasing in a neighborhood with an HOA. One of the best ways to find out is by asking a few of the people who already live there.

14. Look for any water-related problems.

A home in good condition will keep water where it belongs. Exterior moisture should not be making its way inside. Water flowing through the pipes should be staying in those pipes. Any precipitation that falls on and around the property should be directed towards safe areas, like away from your foundation. Your roof should be functioning as intended. Buying somebody's water issues is not what you want. Water issues have a direct correlation to market value, as well as marketability.

15. Have a professional look for the presence of asbestos, mold, and radon.

Asbestos was a major building material up until around 1977. Before you buy a home, you should be aware of the presence of asbestos, because it can drive up the cost of repairs and renovations while driving down the resale value. If you are planning on doing any repair work yourself, it is especially important that you know of asbestos and takes proper precautions if it is present.

Mold is one of the scariest issues with home buyers today and with good reason as it can cause health problems. If you have any respiratory problems, the presence of mold in a home can make them far worse. Any mold remediation that is necessary should be taken care of by the seller.

Radon is an invisible, odorless gas that can be found both in the air and the water. Getting rid of radon in the air is easy and rather inexpensive. Removing radon from water, on the other hand, is much more expensive. On average, the cost to remove radon from the air is around $1000-1300 depending on where you live. Removing radon from water is more like $4000-$7000.

16. Make sure the electrical system is up to par.

Current building codes require modern electrical wiring. Most homes built before the 1930s are not up to standard unless they have been renovated. These old homes use knob and tube wiring, which can be expensive to bring up to code. Keep in mind that many lenders and insurance companies will not work with a buyer if the home has knob and tube wiring due to the hazards it creates.

17. Know your plan for furniture.

If you have furniture you like, you will want to bring it with you. Make sure your new home can accommodate it. Or, if you plan on buying new furniture, you want to purchase a home at a price that leaves you with enough left over to furnish it.

18. Don't stress the wall colors and carpet condition.

Many buyers don't have a vision when looking at homes. As crazy as it sounds there are customers who will turn down a home that meets all the criteria they are looking for because they can't see past the ugly mauve carpeting and the purple and green wall colors.

This is a mistake. One of the easiest things to change about a home is the color of the walls. Paint is inexpensive and can be applied by you after you buy. The same holds true for carpets. While it is always smart for a seller to spend the money to neutralize a home before it goes on the market that doesn't mean you should pass on it!

19. Don't do anything to affect your financial situation.

Your pre-approval is based on the information given at the time of your application. Any changes, like getting a different job or taking out a car loan, can result in denial of the loan request when you go to purchase a house.

Making a large purchase is not a prudent thing to do when buying a home. This is one of the primary reasons buyers can be denied a mortgage after being pre-approved.

20. Know the potential growth of your investment.

Buying a fixer-upper in an area that is growing more popular offers the possibility of an increase in the value of your home. In contrast, buying the nicest house in the area may not have much of an upside.

Before Buying Summary Checklist

Questions to ask before buying a house

- ________ Will the windows need to be replaced?
- ________ What's the position of the trees around the house?
- ________ Have there ever been any pest infestations?
- ________ Does the neighborhood have sidewalks?
- ________ Is the house outdated?
- ________ Does the house have any funny smells?
- ________ Does the ground seem to slope?
- ________ What are the cars like in the neighborhood?
- ________ What are the neighbors like?
- ________ How much will the utilities run?
- ________ Are there any sex offenders in the neighborhood?
- ________ Is there radon gas in the house?
- ________ How do the schools rate in the area?
- ________ Are the gutters in good condition?
- ________ How much noise do you hear in the neighborhood?
- ________ Have there been any new renovations on the house?
- ________ What would my commute to work look like?
- ________ How old are the appliances?
- ________ Are there bathroom vents?
- ________ What are the toilets like?
- ________ What is the humidity level?
- ________ Did the seller have pets?
- ________ Are some parts of the house a different temperature?
- ________ What's the neighborhood like at night?
- ________ How much are the property taxes?
- ________ What are the monthly maintenance and utility costs?
- ________ Has there ever been a broken pipe or sewer backup?
- ________ How old is the roof?
- ________ Are there warranties on the appliances?
- ________ Are there parking restrictions around the house?
- ________ Does the house have any kind of unusual history?

Essential Points You Should do Before Buying a House

- Double check the facts
- Know the Value of the home
- Interview multiple lenders and agents
- Consider all the expenses
- Check for outstanding permits
- Hire a home inspector
- Check for asbestos
- Check the wiring
- Check for water issues
- Settle on a price you are comfortable with
- Consider the HOA's
- Review your credit score
- Get pre-approval
- Find a local Realtor
- Avoid financial changes
- Don't get to hung up on the small stuff
- Envision a fresh coat of paint
- Consider your existing furniture
- Focus on the Kitchen and Bathrooms
- Consider your investment potential
- Be patient

Tips Before Buying a House

- Know your credit score
- Get prequalified
- Shop the lender
- Know every expense
- Know what you want
- Work with a Neighborhood Realtor
- Understand the actual value of the property you are buying
- Buy what you are comfortable paying for
- Verify all the facts
- Try to see yourself in the home
- Use a reputable home inspector
- Make sure all renovations are up to code
- Make sure you read the HOA guidelines
- Look for water-related problems
- Check for asbestos, radon, and mold
- Make sure electrical is up to date
- Plan your furniture layout
- Don't worry about the current carpet or paint
- Don't make financial purchases or alter your credit
- Understand the potential growth of your investment

CHAPTER

3

In this chapter:

10 Things to Watch for When Buying a House

18 Open House Red Flags

12 House-Hunting Tips to Help You Make the Right Choice

6 Things Homebuyers wished they'd known before buying their 1st House

10 Things You Absolutely Need To Know About Buying a Home

20 Things to Consider Beyond the Inspection

Checklists

THINGS TO LOOK FOR WHEN BUYING A HOUSE

10 Things to Watch for When Buying a House

Buying a house can be full of excitement, stress and planning, but hopefully the big payoff will be that you are living in the house of your dreams at the end of the day. Here are 10 things to watch for when buying a house.

1. Recognize a roof in need of repair

   Check out what's happening on top of the house. Does the roof look relatively new or is it caving in? A newer roof could mean a lower homeowners insurance rate. A roof made of an especially sturdy material is better equipped to defend against wind and hail and can possibly save you from a potential claim.

2. Don't judge a room by its paint job

   When you step inside, focus on the structure— aging appliances, loose wires — and tune out any freshly painted walls or upscale decor. The foundation will be there long after the paint starts chipping.

3. Take its temperature

   When you're buying a house, keep in mind: if it looks rickety or old, it probably is. Heating and cooling systems are expensive to fix and replace, and inefficient ones can eat away at your utility bills. Make sure the furnace is up to date and in good repair.

4. Decide on your deal breakers

   Aside from the basics, like quality windows and countertops, think about the purpose of your home and the requirements for your lifestyle, like storage for a large book collection or a big backyard for barbecuing. It can also be a good idea to look for a home with an extra bedroom if you're planning on kids or guests. And if you like to entertain it might be a good idea to look for a house with an entertainment area.

5. Plumbing: what's underneath

   When you're in the kitchen, get underneath the sink and examine those pipes. Check for leaks, water damage, and mold. Not only is mold unsightly and foul-smelling, but it can also cause health problems. If you live with a baby, an elderly person, or someone with asthma, you'll want to be especially careful not to move in to a home with mold.

6. Check out the land

   Don't just look at the building — examine the area around it. Is the house in an area prone to flooding or wildfires? Is the driveway shared with another property? If there are fences, have they been built and positioned properly? When you buy a house, you can't afford to ignore its surroundings.

7. Pay attention to the smells

   Do you smell sewage, gas, or anything equally unpleasant? Sewage systems in older homes can sometimes get clogged or damaged by tree roots. There are sewer or plumbing companies that can send a camera through the pipes to detect any breaks or blockages. Pay attention to pet odors, cigarettes, and mildew.

8. Invest in a well-insulated house

   Check the attic, water pipes, and heating ducts to make sure they're properly insulated. This can reduce heating and cooling costs and keep you comfortable in summer and winter. Double-paned windows can also save you money down the road. Plus, they can help soundproof your place from outside noise.

9. Get your hands on everything

   Turn on every faucet and light switch, open every window and door, flush the toilets, even taste the water. You need to pay attention and know how everything works by putting your hands on them. That way, you can address problem areas and see if there's a cost-effective solution.

10. Have a home inspection done

    There's only so much you can do with your own 5 senses. You'll also want to enlist a professional to ensure the foundation is solid and the wiring is up to code. Home inspectors can even check for lead paint and wood-eating pests.

18 Open House Red Flags

While most home buyers spend their time at an open house passively observing the layout of the rooms and the name brands on the kitchen appliances, smart buyers know the things that are really important to look for when buying a home.

In competitive markets, you'll often walk into an open house that has been deep cleaned, upgraded, and staged with stylish furniture, so you shouldn't be overly impressed by a house that looks and smells nice. This is an opportunity to look beyond the pictures you saw online and figure out if the property is worth seeing again—or if you should move on and never look back.

▶ Red flag No. 1: Smells

Take a deep whiff in every room you enter, and look closely at walls, ceilings, and flooring for signs of pet accidents, mildew, or smoke.

▶ Red flag No. 2: Poor tiling

Inspect the tile in kitchens and bathrooms. If the gaps or tiles are slightly uneven, it may indicate a DIY job. Lazy tiling could indicate that multiple fixes might have been done on the fly, which can add up to big bucks in potential repair costs.

▶ Red flag No. 3: Foundation issues

Most houses have hairline cracks, which just indicate the house is settling into its position, but *large* gaps signal a bigger issue with the foundation. Other areas to observe are sticking doors or windows, visible cracks above window frames, and uneven floors. How do you know if the floors are uneven? Roll a marble from one side to the other.

▶ Red flag No. 4: Foggy or Nonfunctioning Windows

Check for water in between double-paned windows and make sure all the windows are functional.

▶ Red flag No. 5: Nearby water

That creek might look picturesque now, but it won't when it comes cascading through your back door. Unpredictability of weather means that it's vital to consider the possibility of flooding. It has been known that some people are unable to insure their house against flood risk, which can create giant damage bills on a regular basis.

- Red flag No. 6: Bad windows

Take a second to pull back the curtains to check for lopsided frames, and then give the windows a tug to make sure they slide easily. If they stick, it could be a sign of foundation issues, or just poor installation.

- Red flag No. 7: Mold

To detect possible signs of mold while wandering through an open house, discreetly open bathroom and sink cabinets to take a look around water pipes or drains. Even small black or gray spots indicate that more serious issues may be lurking. You can also check the caulking around faucets and tubs for black spots, and look for patches on the ceiling.

- Red flag No. 8: Water damage

A musty odor can indicate water damage, even if you don't see standing water. Check walls and ceilings for water lines; they likely indicate flooding from a leak or a burst pipe that may have caused internal damage. Also, take a look at exposed piping in basements or laundry rooms, and check for rust, water stains, or leaking.

- Red flag No. 9: Cosmetic enhancements

That one freshly painted wall could be an accent wall, or it could be hiding something like a patch of mold. Lift up area rugs to check hardwood flooring, making sure they're not stained or damaged by pets.

- Red flag No. 10: Improper ventilation

Without adequate interior ventilation, moisture sticks around which can create mold and increase allergies. Look for condensation on windows or slightly bubbled or peeling paint around windows, doors, or vents. This can indicate moisture in the walls and ceiling drywall.

The point is to be attentive when you walk through an open house. Even though your home inspector is likely to detect many of these problems down the line, being attentive to these red flags in an open house ensures that you're not wasting your time or money on a home that isn't the one for you.

- Red flag No. 11: Peeling Paint

Peeling paint can be a sign of more than just an old paint job — sometimes, it's caused by rot or moisture penetration.

A property inspection should identify any rot and reveal any windows or seals that aren't watertight, including in the roof. But these inspections are costly. A home inspection might cost you between $300 and $500 but can vary depending on the home's size, age and location, according to the U.S. Department of Housing and Urban Development.

If the home inspection reveals the home has rot or water damage, ask the seller to pay for the repairs.

▶ Red Flag No. 12: Unfinished Construction

Sometimes, a house is listed before renovations are complete. It's possible the owner ran out of money or ran into issues with the property that prevented the renovation from being finished on time. If you are interested in learning more about the status of the house, call the contractor with any questions—don't ask the seller because you want to try to get neutral information.

Make sure your lender will still finance a home with unfinished construction work. According to Realtor.com, construction loans are riskier than standard home loans, and you will need excellent credit and at least a 20 percent to 25 percent down payment.

Weigh this decision carefully because you might end up jumping through extra hoops and spending more than you intended.

▶ Red Flag No 13. Popcorn Ceilings

Popcorn ceilings are not the worst problem to have, but they will need to be addressed. The U.S. Environmental Protection Agency warns that asbestos might be found in "textured paint and patching compounds used on walls and ceilings." Popcorn ceilings can contain asbestos, according to HomeAdvisor.com, which means you might need to fork over extra cash to make your new home safe and healthy.

You might be able to remove the popcorn yourself, but consider hiring a professional to do it for you—especially if asbestos is a factor. Popcorn ceiling removal can cost $1 to $2 per square foot, with the average homeowner forking over approximately $1,439, according to HomeAdvisor.

Ultimately, a thorough, professional home inspection should unveil any red flags with your potential new home. Once you have an idea of what you could be getting yourself into, you'll have to weigh the pros, cons and costs of inheriting those issues. Ensuring your home meets safety regulations should be your top priority.

▶ Red Flag No. 14: Disjointed Additions

Have you ever visited an open house that looked like it was pieced together? Maybe some of the rooms weren't exactly aligned or were comprised of various building materials. These kinds of discrepancies can indicate that space was added on to the original property.

Additions, like sunrooms or a master suite, can add a lot of value to a property—if they are done well. But sometimes, this kind of work is done by novices who don't get the proper permits, consider how the extra space will affect the structure, or correctly hook up electrical and plumbing systems.

Ask the listing agent about the house's history. A good agent should know when any additions were constructed and if permits were acquired. If the agent isn't sure, which could be a red flag, look up the information through city records.

▶ Red Flag No. 15: Deferred Maintenance

During the open house, look for signs of deferred maintenance like broken fixtures, cracked masonry, outdated electrical outlets, sticky doors or unusual drafts. These issues can be signs that the owner has not kept up the home — a mistake that can cost you.

If you love the house, try negotiating with the owner to have him either make the repairs or credit you the cost of hiring professionals to fix the problems.

▶ Red Flag No 16: Multiple Homes for Sale in the Same Area

The house you are looking at might be a perfect fit, but what about the neighborhood? Multiple homes for sale on one street could be a sign that residents aren't happy with the area.

Take a tour of the community, and look for signs of a thriving neighborhood, such as well-kept homes, flourishing businesses, and an abundance of sidewalks and streetlights. If you see any neighbors, ask them how long they've lived there and how they like the area.

▶ Red Flag No 17: Rooms That Are off Limits

Sellers try to do this on a regular basis, especially during open houses. They may have a laundry list of reasons why they don't want to show random strangers what is behind the door, but for a potential buyer, this should increase their concern. Talk to the sellers to try to find out why the room is blocked. Investigate.

▶ Red Flag No 18: Property Neglect

Broken light fixtures, damaged floors, leaking faucets—potential buyers are not going to be interested in a home that has a long list of things to fix. Seeing smaller items in disrepair can lead a buyer to wonder about the state of big-ticket items like the foundation, plumbing, septic system, or roof. Basic fixtures are inexpensive to replace and give a newly remodeled, well-cared-for feeling.

12 House-Hu nting Tips to Help You Make the Right Choice

In the hunt for that perfect house, it's easy to get swept away by a home's most charming details and play down the important things.

These 12 tips can help you stay organized and focused on the important things during your house hunt.

1. Set your priorities. Before taking a look at any houses, sit down and write out everything you want in a home, with input from all members of the household. Then choose your top five, or must-haves.

   Once you start looking, all sorts of charming features are bound to sway you; keeping your priorities list close at hand can help you stay on track.

2. Make a comparison chart. After you have seen a dozen or more houses, it becomes very difficult to keep track of the features in each one. Make things a little easier by creating your own comparison chart or checklist to bring along to each home, and make notes on it during or immediately after each tour.

   Beyond the basics (beds and baths) consider including notes on landscaping, the condition of the roof and exterior, natural light in each room, storage space and cost per square foot. Consider this chart a personal tool — something you can look back on to help guide your decision making.
3. Walk through once and let yourself soak it all in. When you tour a home for the first time, the excitement can make it difficult to focus on. So wander around and mentally note your first impressions of the space. Once the excitement has died down, take another walk through with intentionality.

4. Then go back to the beginning and start again. Walk back to the front of the house and literally begin your tour again. This time, pull out your clipboard and pen, take your time and approach the home as if you were an inspector rather than a potential buyer.

5. Bring furniture measurements. If every room in the house presents problems with your current furniture situation, you could effectively be adding thousands of dollars to the price if you have to purchase new furniture — something that is probably better to know sooner rather than later.

6. Sketch a floor plan. You do not need to have any real drawing skills to make a basic floor plan on paper, and having it to refer to later is priceless. Just do your best. Start at the front door, draw boxes for rooms and mark doors, windows, stairways and openings roughly where they are.

7. Ask to take photos (or even a video). It's amazing how quickly memory fades. Make sure you have backup by creating a floor plan *and* taking photos or a short video tour if possible — it will really give you a full picture of what the house looks like. Be sure to ask the Realtor for permission before taking any photos or video.

8. Open the closets and cupboards. Proper storage is a really important factor in how a home looks and feels when you are living in it. Note the number and size of cupboards and closets throughout the house, and don't be afraid to peek inside. If the current homeowner has them packed, that may be a sign that the house doesn't have enough storage for its size.

9. Lift up the rugs. While this is not something you necessarily want to do during a busy open house, if you are back for a second look and are really considering making an offer, it is important to know what you are getting into. Rugs (and even furniture) can be used to conceal damaged flooring, so you have a right to see what's going on under there. Just let the Realtor know what you want to see, and they should accommodate you.

10. Look high and look low. It is important to get a good look at the house that could be your new home, so make a point of focusing on things outside your usual line of vision. Check out the ceilings, walls, floors, trim, windows, roof and under the sinks.

11. Check out the property at different times of day. If you do come back for a second showing, make it during a different time of day from the open house or first tour. In the evening, notice not only the changes in light, but the atmosphere in the neighborhood. Are people out sitting on porches? Are kids playing outside? Is it noisy? You are bound to learn and discover different things about the house each time.

12. Take a moment to envision how you would use the space. Just because the current owner (or staging company) has the second bedroom set up for guests doesn't mean you can't use it as an office, a home gym or a nursery. Paint colors, furniture arrangements and window treatments can all be swapped out, so use your imagination and really put yourself in the home.

6 Things Homebuyers wished they'd known before buying their 1st House

New homebuyers have made every mistake in the book. They've overpaid, overspent, and bought homes they just could not afford. And most of the time, these critical missteps happen simply because buyers aren't informed or don't ask the right questions. Fortunately these buyer mishaps can be avoided.

Here are 6 of the most common mishaps buyers wish they'd known.

▶ ***Wish they hadn't borrowed the full amount the bank told them they could afford***

Just because you're approved for it doesn't mean you should buy the most expensive house you can. As a general rule, it's wise to take 20% less than what the bank will lend you. Though it may be tempting to take the full amount, knocking a fifth off the loan amount will automatically get you into a house that's more affordable, safeguarding your family and your financial security.

▶ ***Wish they hadn't been talked into the extra-low short-term adjustable rate mortgage***

It is advised to go with a traditional 30- or 15-year fixed loan—and skip adjustable, creative financing, balloon payments, and teaser loans. You never know what life may bring, so having consistent mortgage payments for the entire length of the loan allows you to better predict your ability to pay each month. A fixed mortgage offers confidence that the payment you have today will be the same ten or fifteen years from now, no matter how the market, interest rate, or the economy changes over time.

▶ ***Wish they hadn't used up all their cash to buy the house***

Your home purchasing costs don't stop with the down payment. You have to factor in closing costs, appraisal fees, buyer's broker fees, loan application fees, loan broker fees, structural inspection fees, and so on. The down payment and the closing are the "up-front costs." After that, you've got "ongoing costs," which primarily consist of property taxes, homeowners insurance, hazard insurance, condo, co-op, or HOA fees, and moving expenses. Don't be left with a zero balance in your checking account by the time you get the keys; so factor in these additional costs ahead of time.

- ***Wish they hadn't wasted their time hunting down foreclosures and short sales, only to miss some really good deals***

  Just because it's a distressed property doesn't mean it's a good deal; foreclosures aren't a guaranteed bargain. If you are looking to get a steal (and you want it in a timely manner), avoid short sales, and even some foreclosures. These deals can drag on for months and generally have higher interest rates. And even if the distressed home you're looking at is well-priced, the hoops you'll have to jump through might just have an opportunity cost high enough to offset your monetary cost savings.

- ***Wish they knew that one essential question to ask before buying that condo***

  There's one question that can save you thousands of dollars and help you avoid a condo building (or community with a homeowners association) that will become a money pit: Has there been any discussion of possible future improvements, changes, renovations, or maintenance or any financial difficulties that would result in an assessment or charges to be leveraged against all condo/home owners? Make sure to get the answer in writing. This question is critical because the condo association board must answer honestly or it could be held liable. All condo meetings must provide notes that can be subpoenaed, so any discussion of assessments, current or future, could be proven.

- ***Wish they had talked to the neighbors before buying the house***

  You don't want to wake up to the sounds of barking, yelping dogs that howl and bellow until morning. Chatting with the neighbors can disclose a lot of information.

We all make mistakes when we do something for the first time. It happens, it's normal, but buying a home is one of those things that is just too important to make a mistake. Keep in mind these common mistakes when looking for your dream home.

10 Things You Absolutely Need To Know About Buying a Home

1. Use a trusted realtor. We all know that realtors get a cut of the sales price of a home which makes some buyers hesitant to use a realtor: they believe it drives up the overall cost. Keep in mind that the seller, not the buyer, pays the commission. That means that as a buyer you will not be charged for using a Realtor. A savvy realtor who works for you can protect your interests and guide you through the buying process - from negotiating a price to navigating home inspections.

2. Remember that a house purchase involves a contract. When you're buying a house, there are papers to sign. And more papers to sign. Many of those papers - which are actually contracts - look like "standard" home buying contracts with no room for negotiation. That isn't true. Contracts are meant to be negotiated. You don't have to sign a standard agreement. If you want more time to review your

inspection, wish to waive a radon test or want to make a purchase subject to a mortgage approval, you can make that part of the deal. That's where a savvy realtor can help, so therefore make sure that you use a trusted Realtor to help protect your interests.

3. Don't necessarily buy for the life you have today. Chances are that buying a house will be one of the bigger financial commitments you'll make in your lifetime. Before you agree to buy what you think might be your dream house, consider your long-term plans. Are you planning on staying at your current job? Getting married? Having kids? Depending on the market and the terms of your mortgage, you may not actually pay down any real equity for between five and seven years: if you aren't sure that your house will be the house for you in a few years, you may want to keep looking.

4. Think about commitment. I'm not talking just about your mortgage. When you get married, the laws of your state generally determine how your assets are treated - and ultimately how they're distributed at divorce. The same rules don't necessarily apply when you're not married. That means you need to think long term. When you buy a house with your significant other who is not your spouse, make sure you have an exit plan if things don't go the way you plan. It's a good idea to have an agreement in place with respect to titling, mortgage payments and liability, repairs etc. It is advised to always get it in writing. It is recommended to get professional advice, such as a lawyer.

5. Look beyond paint. It's often the case that your dream house has that one room that you're already fantasizing about changing. It is fairly inexpensive to fix cosmetic issues (a bit of paint or some wallpaper) but making changes to kitchens and baths can be expensive. People tend to focus on the cost of cabinets, appliances and counters but sometimes forget about the cost of labor which can double to triple the cost. That doesn't mean that you should give up on a house in need of a significant fix but you should factor in those costs when determining whether you can afford to buy it.

6. Buy the house you know that you can afford. This can be different from the price that your mortgage company believes that you can afford. Some lenders suggest that you can afford mortgage payments totaling about 1/3 of your gross income but others suggest closer to 28% for housing related costs including mortgage, insurance and taxes. There are a number of factors including your projected income, interest rates, type of mortgage and the market. Ask your mortgage broker to help you to understand.

7. Don't fixate on the purchase price. The purchase price is just one piece of owning a house: be sure to consider all of the costs associated with your potential new home. That includes the cost of insurance, homeowner association fees and real estate taxes - depending on where you live, those can quickly add up. And it's not just home improvements that can cost money: maintenance costs dollars, too. It's a good idea to ask questions about upkeep for extras like swimming pools, fancy heating and cooling systems etc.

8. Consider your student loan debt. Student debt isn't merely an annoyance: it's treated like real debt. A major revision to FHA guidelines in 2015 negatively affects many first-time homebuyers with student

loan debt. Prior to this change, a borrower with student loans deferred for more than 12 months could discount that debt from their liabilities: now, for purposes of determining purchasing power, a borrower is charged with 2% of the outstanding balance of the student loan regardless of deferment status (in a non-FHA, or conventional loan, it's just 1%). If your student loan is in deferment and you're planning on buying a home, consider enrolling in a properly documented income-based repayment plan so you have the documents your lender will need to properly assess your ongoing liability.

9. Don't get carried away by the home mortgage interest deduction. Many taxpayers are tempted to buy more house than they can afford by figuring that they'll save enough with the home mortgage interest deduction to make up for it. The mortgage interest deduction is only deductible if you itemize on your Schedule A: only about 1/3 of taxpayers claim the itemized deduction.

10. You don't have to buy a house. There's no rule that says you have to buy a house by the time you're 35 - or ever. Buying a home is a big decision and while it can be a sound financial investment, it's not for everyone. There is a lot to consider, including the housing market, interest rates, timing and your future plans. You might want more flexibility or mobility, or your career and family plans may be in flux. If you're not sure about a neighborhood, consider renting as a test drive: a realtor can help you with that. Even then, you don't have to pull the switch: there are healthy rental markets throughout the country and in some areas; young professionals are choosing rentals over home buying to preserve cash and remain mobile. Consider all of the facts and then decide the best option for yourself.

20 Things to Consider Beyond the Inspection

Learn what to look for at open houses to
ensure comfort in your new home.

Here are 20 things to look for!

1. Indoor-outdoor flow. The ease with which you can move from indoor to outdoor living areas and back again can make a huge difference in your day-to-day experience of living in a home. If this is important to you, look for French, sliding or accordion glass doors leading from the main living spaces to the outdoors.

2. Size of rooms. Not too big, not too small. Imagine setting up your own furniture in the rooms as you walk through — bring measurements if you can.

3. Interior layout. Like indoor-outdoor flow, the interior layout, or floor plan, can have a big effect on your daily life. Walk through the rooms, imagining your typical day. Are there sharp corners and narrow passages to navigate, or is there an easy, natural flow from one room to the next?

4. Lot grade. The steepness of a lot is in some ways even more important than its size. Think about not just what you want today but what you might want in the future. If down the road you were to decide you wanted to add a deck, an extra room or a backyard studio, would that be possible on your lot?

5. Window size and placement. You can of course add and modify windows, but it's not the cheapest change to make to a house. It would be a good idea to look for a home with ample, well-placed windows.

6. Amount of natural light. Once you have a few homes on your list that are strong contenders, make appointments to give them a second look at a different time of day. This will give you a fuller picture of what the light is like in the home.

7. Regional weather considerations. Will you live somewhere with cold winters? You may want to put an attached garage, covered entrances and an easy-to-shovel driveway on your checklist. Those in warm climates may want to focus on shaded walkways and cooling trees.

8. House orientation on lot. The way a house is positioned on its lot affects how much natural light it gets and can influence heating and cooling bills as well. A south-facing home will maximize natural light—though a north-facing home can be just as bright if the main living space is in the back of the home and there are ample windows all around. In hot climates a north-facing home with deep eaves may be preferable to keep your house cooler.

9. Driveway length and width. Is the driveway wide enough for your car, boat, motor home?

10. Street parking. Some towns and cities have strange rules and regulations regarding street parking. What do the signs display? Are permits required?

11. Staircase steepness and length. You may not have the slightest problem with stairs now but this is one of those times it's helpful to think about the future. If you think you might ever want or need to take in an elderly relative, or you plan to age in this home, a long, steep staircase may not be the best feature.

12. Architectural details. Great architectural details, like exposed beams, beautiful molding and mantels, will make everything else you do to your home look even better.

13. Heating and cooling systems. If you live somewhere that gets very hot in summer or cold in winter, good heating and cooling systems will make life much more pleasant. And because putting in central air conditioning or heating can cost a fair amount and the work is disruptive, finding a home where it's already in place will save money and hassle.

14. Laundry room location. Is the laundry in a convenient spot, or is it hidden away in a dingy corner of the basement? Since this is a chore that usually needs to be done frequently, having a laundry near a main living area can make life easier.

15. Kitchen features. Ask whoever does most of the cooking in your household to make a wish list for the kitchen. Does he or she prefer to work on a gas stove? If so, be sure to check for one. Ask if the house is connected to a gas line so that you can add your own gas stove. Other things to consider in the kitchen could include its shape or layout, natural light, number of sinks, storage area and overall size.

16. Number of bathrooms. Adding a bathroom is expensive, so choose a home with enough baths to meet your family's needs. Even if you are a household of only one or two people, an extra powder room on the main floor can be a big plus.

17. Ceiling height. Some basement and attic rooms have less than adequate ceiling heights. If someone in your household is tall, bring them along to the open house to make sure the fit in all the rooms is comfortable.

18. Zoning and town ordinances for animals. Could you one day want backyard chickens or another unconventional pet? Check local ordinances before committing to a house, or you may never get the pets you have your heart set on.

19. Closeness of neighbors. Though the general area (city versus suburb) has much to do with how close your neighbors are, there can still be a big difference between how private one house feels over another. If privacy is important to you, be sure to check the views from every window and walk the perimeter of the property to get an idea of how close you will be to your next-door neighbors.

20. The neighborhood. This may be where you started your search, but have you really considered all aspects of your potential new neighborhood? School districts are of course important for families with kids, as well as proximity to work. But you may also want to look to see if the area is conducive for biking or walking and what community amenities (libraries, parks) are nearby and what public transportation is available.

10 Things to watch for when buying a house

Summary Checklist

- ________ Recognize a roof in need of repair
- ________ Don't judge a room by its paint job
- ________ Decide on your deal breakers
- ________ Plumbing—what's underneath
- ________ Check out the land
- ________ Pay attention to the smells
- ________ Invest in a well-insulated house
- ________ Get your hands on everything

Open House Red Flag Summary Checklist

- ________ Red Flag #1 Smells
- ________ Red Flag #2 Poor Tiling
- ________ Red Flag #3 Foundation Issues
- ________ Red Flag #4 Signs of deferred maintenance
- ________ Red Flag #5 Nearby water
- ________ Red Flag #6 Bad Windows
- ________ Red Flag #7 Mold
- ________ Red Flag #8 Water Damage
- ________ Red Flag #9 Cosmetic enhancements
- ________ Red Flag #10 Improper Ventilation
- ________ Red Flag #11 Peeling Paint
- ________ Red Flag #12 Unfinished Construction
- ________ Red Flag #13 Popcorn Ceilings

__________ Red Flag #14 Disjointed Additions

__________ Red Flag #15 Deferred Maintenance

__________ Red Flag #16 Multiple Homes for Sale in the Area

__________ Red Flag #17 Rooms That Are Off Limits

__________ Red Flag #18 Property Neglect

12 House Hunting Tips Summary Checklist

__________ Set your priorities

__________ Make a comparison chart

__________ Do a thorough walk thru

__________ Start over again

__________ Bring furniture measurements

__________ Sketch a floor plan

__________ Take photos

__________ Open the closets and cupboards

__________ Lift up the rugs

__________ Look high and low

__________ Check out the property at different times of the day

__________ Envision how you will use the space

6 Things Homebuyers wished they'd known before buying Summary Checklist

__________ Not to borrow the full amount offered

__________ To not take the extra low short term adjustable mortgage

__________ Used all of their cash to buy a house

__________ Hadn't wasted their time hunting down foreclosures or short sales

__________ To ask the essential question before buying that condo about HOA

__________ To have talked to the surrounding neighbors

10 Essential Home Buying facts Summary Checklist

__________ Use a trusted realtor

__________ A house purchase involves a contract

__________ Don't buy for the life you have today

__________ Think about the commitment

__________ Look beyond the paint

__________ Buy the house you can afford

__________ Don't fixate on the purchase price

__________ Consider your student loan debt

__________ Know the truth about mortgage interest deduction

__________ You don't have to buy a house

20 Things to consider beyond inspection Summary Checklist

__________ Indoor outdoor flow

__________ Size of the rooms

__________ Interior layout

__________ Lot grade

__________ Window size

__________ Amount of light

__________ Weather considerations

__________ House orientation

__________ Driveway length and width

__________ Street parking

__________ Staircase steepness and length

__________ Architectural details

__________ Heating and cooler systems

__________ Laundry room locations

__________ Kitchen features

__________ Number of bathrooms

__________ Ceiling height

__________ Zoning and town ordinances

__________ Closeness of neighbors

__________ Neighborhood

Quick View scorecard Summary Checklist

__________ Is the house close to important facilities?

__________ Does the house have the right number of rooms to suit your needs?

__________ Are the building and roof structurally sound?

__________ What is neighborhood noise levels like?

__________ Does the house have good natural light?

__________ Does the house have adequate power?

__________ Is there any sign of termite activity?

__________ Are there any planned developments nearby?

__________ Is the garden suitable?

__________ Does the property provide sufficient parking space?

__________ Is the property at risk of flooding?

__________ What will some of the ongoing costs be?

__________ Where are the official property boundaries?

__________ Will you need to do any renovations?

CHAPTER

4

In this chapter:

24 Real Estate Tips

123's of Real Estate

ABC's of Buying a Short Sale Home

21 Real Estate Terms Every Home Buyer Should Understand

Checklists

REAL ESTATE TIPS

24 Real Estate Tips

Tip #1: Decide location versus space before searching for a home

Before shopping for a home, it's important to set your priorities and decide which is more important to you: space or location. If you settle on this in advance, you can make better decisions during the home-buying process and avoid the unsettling feeling of buyer's remorse.

Tip #2: Don't commit before you're ready

Owning a home is a huge commitment. Before buying a home, make sure you know exactly what you're getting into so you can decide if you're financially and personally ready for such a large commitment. In addition to your monthly mortgage payment, figure out how much you'll be paying for property taxes, homeowner's insurance, HOA fees and other monthly costs of owning a home.

Tip #3: Sweat equity can save thousands

If you have the skills, the time and the patience to live with dust and debris for a while, do-it-yourself home improvement projects can save you a big chunk of cash.

Tip #4: A down payment is never a bad investment

Putting some money down is a good idea for any homebuyer because it minimizes your risk and lets you start off with some equity.

Tip #5: The school district will affect home value

Even if you don't have kids, it pays to check out a neighborhood's school district before buying a home, as living in an area with a sought-after school system raises your property value.

Tip #6: A land survey will answer boundary questions

Before making changes to your property, it's a good idea to find out your exact property lines. You can't always rely on the seller's knowledge of the property, so getting a land survey will clear up any uncertainties you have.

Tip #7: Check building plans for the neighborhood

Before buying a home, find out if there are any building plans near your home to avoid surprises after you've moved in.

Tip #8: Fixer Uppers

It takes a special person to see the potential in a home that's in need of serious rehab. If you've got your heart set on buying a dream fixer-upper — but don't have the savings to cover both a down payment *and* a renovation — there are loan products out there that could help you make your dream a reality. Get the facts.

Tip #9: Consider a loan with a built-in reserve

The Federal Housing Administration (FHA) 203(k) rehabilitation loan or Fannie Mae HomeStyle Renovation Mortgage could be good financing options for buyers seeking fixer-uppers. These loans allow you to purchase the home with a reserve that's put in escrow to fund renovations.

One caveat: There are strict guidelines, and it's important to understand how these loans work if you're considering a handyman special.

Tip #10: Dig deeper during inspection

If a problem presents itself during your inspection, address it right away.

Tip #11: Continue negotiating after the inspection

If a flaw is discovered during your home inspection, use it to your advantage. Knowing about the flaws in the property can help you during negotiations to get a price reduction. Even after inspections, you still have another chance to get a great deal. Staying under budget when buying a home gives you extra cash to add the upgrades and decor you want.

Tip #12: Real estate is not a recession-proof investment

Not everything always goes according to plan. Equity buys you options and additional exit strategies, which are important to maintain and nice to have, especially in a downturn economy.

A big part of being recession proof is having the humility to admit that you don't know with certainty how things could play out.

Tip #13: Examine both financial and personal costs of buying

Purchasing a home can require you to make tough personal sacrifices. Before buying a home, think about what kind of personal and financial sacrifices you'll have to make. If affording a home is a stretch right now, it might be better to wait awhile and save up more money.

Tip #14: Read HOA documents before closing

Reading a big stack of papers may seem like a huge hassle, but carefully reviewing your HOA documents is important if you want to avoid unpleasant surprises down the road. Before buying a home in a community with an HOA, read through the covenants, conditions and restrictions (CC&Rs), bylaws and budget and look for anything that could affect you in the future. Also, talk to residents in the complex and get opinions on how well the HOA does its job.

Tip #15: Secure financing before falling in love with a house - Preapproval

A mortgage preapproval is a letter from a lender indicating how much of a loan you can qualify for, issued after the lender has evaluated your financial history — including pulling your credit report and score. With a preapproval letter, you can find a home you can afford by shopping within your means — while showing you're a serious buyer.

Tip #16: Don't spend every dollar you qualify for

By not spending every bit you qualify for, you can open yourself up to more options and better possibilities.

Tip #17: Find smart money

Investigate "smart money" options by getting a loan through a non-profit organization that may have agreements with several lenders to give first-time homebuyers affordable loans. These kinds of opportunities are out there; you just have to look for them. Remember, you still have to be underwritten by the lenders, so be prepared to show your credit history and attend classes and workshops the non-profit group organizes.

Tip #18: Make sure renovations were professionally done

Paying close attention to the aesthetic details of a home is just as important as the structural details when going through an inspection. Oftentimes, do-it-yourself remodelers looking for a quick fix use low-quality materials that turn into a problem for future homeowners. They key is to make sure any renovations were done by a professional contractor using quality materials that are meant to last. Inspecting details up front is very important so you don't find yourself shelling out even more cash later on.

Tip #19: A creative bid strategy helps ensure a good deal

By making an offer on the home, then adding a contingency that would increase $1,000 over any other competing offers up to your maximum price point, you could increase your chance of getting the house with minimal dollars spent over the highest competing offer. Although unconventional, a creative strategy like this can be very effective in today's market, especially when there are competing bids for the property.

Tip #20: Don't overlook the landscaping

Updates to the exterior of a home can add up just as quickly as the interior. If you aren't looking to spend much more on the details once you have found a home, look for a property that already has the amenities and the landscaping that you desire.

Tip #21: A higher price point might save money over time

After making interior and exterior renovations, many homeowners find that their budget has been stretched way beyond what they initially wanted to pay for a home. For this reason, it can be smart to adjust your price point a little to help you save money over time. By paying a little more upfront for a home that has all of the upgrades and extras you want, you won't have to worry about paying for them down the road.

Tip #22: Low-balling doesn't always pay off

Unfortunately, looking for homes at the top of their price range and making lowball offers -- plus asking sellers to contribute to their down payment and closing costs, make offers look weak and may be rejected, outbid or ignored every time. If you find yourself incurring multiple losing bids, a change in strategy maybe in order. By giving a little bit, you can get a lot in return.

Tip #23: Change a bid strategy that's failing

Tweaking your bidding strategy can make the possibility of getting the house you want much more realistic. Try to be smarter, faster and closer to the original asking price in order to put in a competitive bid. The offer should be strong enough to at least hit the seller's base price. The key to remember is if you would like the sellers to do something for you, such as contributing to closing costs or the down payment, then you need to get as close to their asking price as possible.

Tip #24: Save money for a down payment

Take some time to save money for a down payment before buying a home. Your offer will look stronger to the seller, and you'll have more leverage during negotiations.

123's of Real Estate

1. What is Home Warranty Insurance and why do I need it?

   A private insurance program that usually is paid for by the seller that protects the buyer of any unforeseen problems after you move in, such as roofing, heating, air conditioning, pool, appliances, etc.

   If after you move into your new home and after turning on the heating unit, and find out it is working improperly, you may be covered to have it fixed or replaced with Home Warranty Insurance.

2. What are the Tax Benefits of Homeownership?

   When you are figuring out how much you can afford to commit to monthly mortgage payments, don't forget the tax advantages of home ownership. Both property taxes and interest payments on a mortgage for an owner-occupied home are currently tax deductible. As a homeowner, your annual taxable income could be substantially reduced by deducting the payments you make on property taxes and yearly mortgage interest.

   Ask your CPA/Account/Tax Preparer how buying a home would affect your taxes

   Note: In addition to tax advantages, you can also benefit from any increase in the value of your home both through appreciation and improvements you add for your own comfort and enjoyment.

3. What is Title Insurance and why do I need it?

   The deed to your new home is not enough to ensure clear title; it is merely an instrument whereby the seller transfers right of ownership to you. It doesn't prove that the person described as the seller is actually the clear owner of the property, and it does not eliminate claims or rights that others may have in the property.

   A title company conducts a thorough search and evaluation of the Public Records, looking for situations that may cloud the title to your new home, such as:

   - Are all taxes and special assessments paid?
   - Does anyone have special rights to the property that would limit ownership
   - Has the death of a former owner or the filing of a will affect title
   - Are there undisclosed heirs or spouses of the seller
   - Are there any lawsuits or claims recorded against the property

   By obtaining Title Insurance, you will protect yourself from these possible disasters.

   See your Real Estate agent for references.

4. What are the 8 Ways to Hold Title?

   1. Single Man or Single Woman—A man or woman who is not legally married.
   2. An Unmarried Man or Unmarried woman—A man or woman who is legally divorced.
   3. A Married Man or Married Woman—As his or Her Sole and Separate Property

4. Community Property—Property acquired by husband and wife together
5. Joint Tenancy—Property owned by 2 or more persons with equal shares
6. Tenancy in Common—The owners own undivided interests—not equal shares
7. Trust—The trust holds legal and equitable title to the property
8. Community Property with Right of Survivorship—Community property of a husband and wife, when expressly declared in the transfer document to be community property with the right of survivorship, and which may be accepted in writing on the face of the document by a statement signed or initialed by the grantees, shall upon the death of one of the spouses, pass to the survivor the full property.

5. What is Mello-Roos?

Under Mello-Roos Community Facilities Act, landowners put up their land as collateral so that public agencies, like a school district, could raise money to pay for vital basic public facilities. The public agency forms a Mello-Roos Community District that sells bonds to fund the construction of these new public facilities. A bond allows for payment over a specific amount of time through special taxes levied on property owners in that particular district. Mello-Roos taxes are paid by the County Tax Collector as part of the normal property tax system.

The payment of an assessment is ordinarily spread over a period of years requiring the annual payment of principal and interest. In some instances, the payments are spread on the secured tax roll and collected with the installments of county real property taxes. In some cases, payment of the special assessment must be made to a different county or municipal office.

6. What is Supplemental Property Taxes?

Supplemental property taxes only affect individuals who are buying property or initiating new construction. After the purchase or new construction is complete, the new owner will receive a bill for supplemental property taxes which will become a lien against the property as of the date ownership changes or upon the date of completion of new construction.

The total supplemental assessment will be prorated based on the number of months remaining until June 30, the end of the tax year.

All supplemental taxes are payable in two equal installments. The taxes are due on the date the bill is mailed and are delinquent on specified dates depending on the month the bill is mailed.

7. When are Property Taxes due?

January 1—Assessment date

April 15—Last day to file for 100% Veterans or Homeowners Exemption

July 1—Current fiscal Tax year begins

November 1—First installment due (1st installment—July 1—December 31

December 1—Last day to file for 80% Veterans or Homeowners Exemption

January 1—Calendar Year Begins

February 1—Second Installment due (2nd installment—January 1 to June 30)

April 10—Second Installment Becomes Delinquent at 5pm

June 30—Property tax may become defaulted.

Remember: Property may be sold at public auction after 5 years of delinquent taxes!

8. What is Escrow and How does it work?

Escrow is the process by which the interest of all parties in a real estate transaction are protected, ensuring that all conditions of the sale have been met before property and money change hands.

The escrow holder is a neutral third party that maintains the escrow account and impartially oversees the escrow process, making sure all conditions of the sale are properly met.

9. What is a Home Inspection and why do I need it?

The Physical Inspection clause in your Purchase Contract, when initialed by both Parties, allows the right to have the property thoroughly inspected. This is done through a General Home Inspection. While Home Inspectors are not currently required to have a license, most are, or have been General Contractors. The inspection and the resulting report will provide an overall assessment of the present condition of the property.

Home inspection covers items such as exterior siding, paint, flooring, appliances, water heater, furnace, electrical service, plumbing and other visible features of the property.

The Buyer typically pays for this service. Fees range from $200—600.

(Depending on Inspection Company and square footage of property)

10. What is A Structural Pest Control Inspection and why do I need it?

Often referred to as a "Termite Report" the Structural Pest Control Inspection is conducted by a licensed Inspector. In addition to actual termite damage, the Pest Report will indicate any type of weed-destroying organism that may be present, including fungi (sometimes called, "dry rot").

Section I Conditions

Most pest reports classify conditions as Section I or Section II items. Section I Conditions are those which are "active" or currently causing damage to the property. Generally, Section I items need to be corrected before a lender will make a loan on a home.

Section II Conditions

Areas that are not currently causing damage, but are likely to, if left unattended. A type Section II item is a plumbing leak where the moisture has not yet caused fungus decay.

Who Pays?

The Purchase Contract will specify who is responsible for the cost of the inspection and making these corrections. This is a negotiable item. The Seller usually pays for Section I & if Section II is considered it is usually paid for by the Buyer.

11. What is a Tax Lien?

A lien by definition is a claim against an item, which affects the ability to transfer ownership by another party, which utilizes that item as security for repayment of a loan, or other claim. Property taxes are also called ad valorem taxes, and are defined as county assessed taxes on real property within the county boundaries. So when you see ad valorem taxes you can know that they're talking about property taxes.

Every piece of real estate is subject to property taxes; vacant land, raw land, land with buildings on it. Everything is subject to property taxes. The tax rate for each property is based on a combination of property value and the county's estimated budget for the year. That's why the assessed value of the home is almost always different than the fair market value.

The county uses those property taxes to fund things like the fire department, police department, road signs, streets, development projects, schools, teachers, etc. That's the reason this investment exists, because property taxes are the primary source of income for the county government. If there weren't property taxes then the county governments would be broke. They need that money to operate. Therefore, they created this strategy to make sure they get their money.

Many property owners just pay their property taxes along with their mortgage; but sometimes the property owner doesn't have a mortgage or maybe the owner passed away, so the property owner fails to pay those property taxes before the due date. Instead of raising taxes for those that actually pay taxes, the county places a tax lien on the property. The tax lien affects the ability to transfer ownership by another party, which utilizes that item as security for repayment of a loan or other claim. After the tax lien is issued it gives the county the ability to collect the debt in another way, through tax lien certificates.

12. Advantages of Homesteading Your Property

In certain states, homeowners can take advantage of what's called a homestead exemption. Basically, a homestead exemption allows a homeowner to protect the value of her principal residence from creditors and property taxes. A homestead exemption also protects a surviving spouse when the other homeowner spouse dies. State homestead exemptions often have four features, including the well-known property-tax exemption on a portion of a home's assessed value.

A homeowner's understanding when it comes to homesteading their property most often has to do with the property-tax exemption. Generally, this advantage of homesteading pertains to shielding a portion of a home's value from property taxes. Often, a typical homesteading advantage is that it'll exempt the first $25,000 to $75,000 of a home's assessed value from all property taxes. With a $50,000 homesteading exemption, you'll only owe property taxes on the home's remaining assessed value.

With a homestead exemption, your home is shielded from a forced sale to satisfy creditors. For example, the lender financing your automobile can't force the sale of your home if you default on your auto loan. Before homestead exemptions, creditors could and often did try to seize a homeowner's property to satisfy all kinds of debts. Homestead exemptions, however, don't normally shield your home from forced sale in mortgage foreclosures or from defaulted property taxes.

In order to declare a homestead on your home, it must be your principal residence. In California, homestead exemptions apply only to real property. You won't be able to declare your house boat or motor home a homestead under certain state's homesteading laws. Your homestead exemption and its advantages last until you effectively abandon the homestead, too. Commonly, you abandon an old homestead when you declare another home your new homestead.

ABC's of Buying a Short Sale Home

Buyers pursue short sales to get a good deal because they believe buying a short sale will present an excellent opportunity to buy really cheap. So when you see a price listed for a home that you think is too low for the neighborhood, before you jump on that price, ask your agent to call the listing agent to find out if the home is a short sale.

It's not as simple as you may think and a very limited number can close in 30 days or less.

A. What is a Short Sale?

A successful short sale means the seller's lender is willing to accept a discounted payoff to release an existing mortgage. Just because a property is listed with short sale terms does not mean the lender will accept your offer, even if the seller accepts it. That's because sellers need to qualify for a short sale. If their agent sells very few short sales, that's a red flag.

Be aware that the seller need not be in default -- to have stopped making mortgage payments—before a lender will consider a short sale. A lender may consider a short sale if the seller is current but the value has fallen. The seller may have over-encumbered, owe more than the home is worth, so a discounted price might bring the price in line with market value, not below it.

B. Make sure that you check the Public Records

Do your research before making an offer to purchase. Your agent can find out who is on title, whether a foreclosure notice has been filed and how much is owed to the lender(s). This is important because it will help you to determine how much to offer.

Note that banks are not under duress to accept a short sale so the offer needs to be reasonable. If there are two loans, you could have a problem. The first mortgage lender's position is protected by the second lender, unless the second lender does not want to foreclose.

C. Hire an Agent with Short Sale Experience

It's one strike against you if the listing agent has never handled a short sale, but it's even worse if your own agent has no experience in that arena. Don't go into a situation where you have an Agent that is not experienced with Short sales. You need an experienced short sale agent who can anticipate surprises and stop problems from happening.

An agent with experience in short sales will help to expedite your transaction and protect your interests. You don't want to miss any important details due to inexperience or find out your transaction is not going to close on time because no one bothered to follow up in a timely manner.

D. Qualifying the Property and Seller for a Short Sale

A lender is unlikely to agree to a short sale unless the seller has no equity and is unable to repay the difference between your sales price and the existing loans. Sellers need to provide a hardship letter to the lender. Sellers may also owe taxes on the amount of debt that is forgiven.

E. Submit Documentation and Purchase Offer to Lender

Once the seller has accepted your offer, the listing agent will get it to the lender for approval. You do not have a deal until the lender accepts. Also, the lender will want a copy of your earnest money deposit and proof of funds. Do not be astonished if the lender asks you to increase your sales price.

In addition, the lender will want to see that you have your own loan available and you are preapproved. Send them a current preapproval letter dated within the last 30 days. It will help if your agent sends a list of comparable sales that support the price you are offering to pay for the home.

F. Give the Short Sale Lender Time to Respond

Make your offer contingent upon the lender's acceptance. Give the lender a time frame in which to respond, after which, you will be free to cancel.

Some lenders submit short sales to a committee, but most can make a decision within two weeks to three months. The listing agent should have the appropriate contact information for the lender. As a buyer, you cannot contact the lender nor can your agent, so be patient.

G. Understand Short Sale Commissions

Regardless of the commission, the seller has agreed to pay, the lender is the entity approving the commission. Although the seller is not keeping any of the money, the seller still pays the commission from the proceeds of sale. The lender will likely negotiate the commission directly with the listing broker, who will then share the commission with your agent.

If you have signed a buyer's broker agreement with your agent, ask if the agent will waive the difference due or you might have to pay it out of your pocket. Some brokers feel it is unfair to penalize the agent, but the lender is calling the shots.

H. Reserve the Right to Conduct Inspections

Generally, the lender will not allow a seller to pay for customary items that a traditional seller would pay. These include home protection plans for the buyer, roof / pest / termite inspections and pest completions. A buyer will be asked to purchase the property "as is," which means no repairs.

I. Be Patient & don't be discouraged

Shorts sales can be a tedious, complicated process however if you are successful—you will reap a huge savings. So hang in there and be patient.

21 Real Estate Terms Every Home Buyer Should Understand

Before you even begin looking for a home, here are 21 home buying terms you should understand.

1. Acceptance

This is an agreement to the terms of an offer on a home. If the seller decides to accept the offer, you are both considered under contract. If you try to back out after this point, you face consequences that can include losing any deposit or earnest money you might have fronted.

2. APR

This represents your interest rate each year. The APR on a mortgage must include any fees you pay upfront, including loan origination fees. Your average compound interest and fees over the term of the loan are expressed as a percentage that you can use to compare offers from different lenders.

3. ARM

An adjustable rate mortgage is one with an interest rate that changes as market conditions change. A new rate is often set at regular intervals, such as twice a year or once a year. If you choose an ARM, read the terms, since many of these mortgages put caps on the top interest rate.

4. Appraisal

When you decide to buy a home, the lender wants to know what the home is worth. Lenders don't want to provide a loan for an amount that exceeds the value of the home. An appraisal is a process that determines the value of your home, and it includes factors such as the condition of the property, location, upgrades to the home, and selling prices of similar homes in the neighborhood.

5. Closing

This is the formal and final transfer of a home's ownership between parties.

6. Closing Costs

These are all the costs that you pay as part of the buying process, beyond the cost of the property. Sometimes, the seller pays a portion of the closing costs. Some of the expenses included in closing costs include appraisal fees, credit check fees, escrow fees, points, loan origination fees, and any other fees. All of your costs should be spelled out and itemized in the paperwork.

7. Contingency

If certain terms aren't met, a contingency item in the contract allows you to get out of completing the purchase. One of the most common contingencies — and one that you should make sure is included in your contract — is the ability to void the contract if the home you plan to buy doesn't pass its home inspection.

8. Counter Offer

This is a way to void an original offer. This is often used by a seller when your offer is considered too low. You might offer $200,000, and the seller might come back with $225,000. You then need to decide whether or not you will accept the counter offer.

9. Credit Report

Your credit report is a history of all of your credit dealings. All of your loans will be included. Lenders look at your credit report for an idea of what you owe, and where your finances stand. You normally have to cover the fee the lender pays to pull your credit report. Realize, too, that the lender will get a report from each of the three major bureaus. Each agency offers a score based on the information in the report. Normally, the middle score carries the greatest weight with regard to decisions about your loan.

10. Earnest Money

A buyer pays this money as an indication that he or she is serious about the transaction. You pay this money as you enter into the agreement to buy. The remainder of the money owed for the house is paid at closing (usually with funds borrowed from a lender). If you fail to complete the purchase, the seller gets to keep the earnest money.

11. Equity

Basically, this is the amount of ownership you have in your home. It is found by subtracting what you owe on your mortgage from the market value of your home. If your home is worth $200,000 and you owe $175,000, you have $25,000 equity — or ownership — in your home. If you owe more than your home is worth, you are said to have negative equity.

12. Escrow

During large purchases, a third party is often involved in order to manage the funds. Your money is held in escrow so that the seller can see that you have it — and that you are ready to pay. Then, once the paperwork is signed and you have the title/deed in your name, the funds are released. Using a trusted third party can smooth the process.

13. Fixed Rate Mortgage

With this type of mortgage, the interest rate remains the same throughout the term of the loan. No matter what happens with the markets, the interest rate remains the same.

14. Homeowners' Association

Some neighborhoods have associations designed to encourage certain behaviors and cultivate a specific feeling. These are often associated with condo communities and gated communities, but many open subdivisions have them as well. You pay fees meant to help with certain upkeep, and you agree to abide by rules about home appearance and noise, and other items. Before buying a home, make sure you understand the rules associated with the local homeowners' association.

15. LTV

This is the term that denotes how much equity you have in your home. Loan-to-Value looks at how much you owe as a percentage of the value of your home. If your home is worth $200,000, and you owe $150,000, your LTV is 75%.

16. MLS

A multiple Listing Service allows real estate professionals to see all the details related to a house.

17. Mortgage Broker

A Mortgage Broker is a lending agent who has access to a number of different loan programs. A mortgage broker is paid a commission and can help you compare numerous mortgage options.

18. PITI

A term that is used to denote principal, interest, taxes, and insurance — the major costs associated with homeownership and included in many monthly home payments.

19. PMI

Private mortgage insurance is required if you don't have a down payment of at least 20%. PMI is designed to protect the lender, and if you default, the lender is reimbursed by the insurance. Once your home reaches 80% LTV, you aren't required to pay PMI premiums anymore.

20. Real Estate Agent

Someone licensed to show properties and facilitate selling transactions.

21. Title

Indication of ownership of the home, usually recorded on a deed. A report, verifying that the title is "clean" and without liens against the property, or that there are no other claims on the property, is required before the purchase.

24 Real Estate Tips Summary Checklist

Tip #1 Decide location vs. space

Tip #2 Don't commit before your ready

Tip #3 Sweat equity can save thousands

Tip #4 A down payment is never a bad investment

Tip #5 The school district will affect home value

Tip #6 A land survey will answer boundary questions

Tip #7 Check building plans for the neighborhood

Tip #8 Fixer upper—get the facts

Tip #9 Consider a loan with built-in reserve

Tip #10 Dig deeper during inspections

Tip #11 Continue negotiation after inspection

Tip #12 Real Estate is not a recession-proof investment

Tip #13 Examine both financial and personal costs of buying

Tip #14 Read HOA documents carefully

Tip #15 Secure financing before falling in love with the house

Tip #16 Don't spend every dollar you qualify for

Tip #17 Find smart money

Tip #18 Make sure renovations were professionally done

Tip #19 A creative bid strategy helps ensure a good deal

Tip #20 Don't overlook the landscaping

Tip #21 A higher price point might save money over time

Tip #22 Low-balling doesn't always pay off

Tip #23 Change a bid strategy that's failing

Tip #24 Save money for a down payment

123's of Real Estate Summary Checklist

- What is Home Warranty Insurance?
- What are the Tax Benefits of Homeownership?
- What is Title Insurance?
- What are the 8 Ways to Hold Title?
- What is Mello-Roos?
- What is Supplemental Property Taxes?
- When are Property Taxes due?
- What is Escrow?
- What is a Home Inspection?
- What is a Structural Pest Control Inspection?
- What is a Tax lien?
- Homesteading

ABC's of Buying a Short Sale Summary Checklist

- What is a Short Sale?
- Make sure that you check the public records
- Hire an Agent with Short Sale experience
- Qualifying the Property and Seller for a Short Sale
- Submit Documentation and Purchase offer to the Lender
- Give the Short Sale Lender time to respond
- Understand Short Sale Commissions
- Reserve the Right to conduct inspections

- Be patient—don't be discouraged

21 Real Estate Terms to know Summary Checklist

- Acceptance
- APR
- ARM
- Appraisal
- Closing
- Closing Costs
- Contingency
- Counter Offer
- Credit Report
- Earnest Money
- Equity
- Escrow
- Fixed Rate Mortgage
- Homeowners Association
- LTV
- MLS
- Mortgage Broker
- PITI
- PMI
- Real Estate Agent
- Title

THINGS TO DO AFTER YOU BOUGHT YOUR HOUSE

CHAPTER

5

In this chapter:

New home checklist: 12 things homeowners should do right away

19 Ways to Immediately Save Money

123's of moving in

Checklists

New home checklist: 12 things homeowners should do right away

The weeks leading up to a home purchase can be pretty stressful. Between the home inspection and finalizing your financing, you also have to start packing up your entire life and maybe arranging for movers—or even selling your old house under a tight timeline. Then there's the actual closing.

But after closing, the real fun begins. Here are a few small, manageable-but-productive tasks during your first week of home ownership that can make you feel way more in control of things during a period that can easily spiral into feeling overwhelmed.

Here is a checklist of simple things you can and should take care of when you first move into your new home:

1. Take a few days off.

   The first week or two in your new home will be full of phone calls, fixing things, unpacking, and waiting—for deliveries, contractors, and Internet installers. Trying to squeeze all that in around your job will only make it more stressful.

   You just bought a house — it's a big deal, and something you'll probably only do a few times in a lifetime. So take some time off so as not to overwhelm yourself.

2. Try to do any improvements or repairs you can before moving in.

   Whether you do it yourself or hire a professional, it's easier to do work on a house when it's empty of moving parts like your family. This is especially true for those projects best done without furniture in the way, such as interior painting, plastering, or sanding and refinishing hardwood floors.

And if your home needs some work behind the walls — such as updating knob-and-tube wiring or replacing rusted-out pipes — do it before you get settled in if you can.

3. Change your address and set up utilities.

As soon as possible, alert the post office that you've changed your address, so they can forward mail to your new home. However, that service only lasts for a few months, so you should also start changing your address on all of your important accounts, such as your workplace benefits, bank accounts, credit cards, car and health insurance, magazine subscriptions, and memberships.

Also, call up the gas and electric companies and tell them you've moved. In most cases they'll just transfer your account to your new address. You can often do the same with your cable or Internet provider, too, if you're moving within the same service area. Otherwise, investigate your local options and call to set up service while you're home getting settled.

4. Clean

Before you unpack, and ideally before the furniture arrives, thoroughly clean your new home, or hire a house cleaner to do a one-time deep cleaning.

Vacuum and wash carpets (rent a carpet cleaner if you need one), sweep and mop the floors, bleach the entire bathroom, clean the fridge and the oven and all the sinks, and wipe down all your cabinets, drawers, shelves, and closets.

5. Change the locks.

Even if you like and trust the previous owner, there's no way of knowing how many copies of your house key are floating around—or who has them. A new door hardware set is well worth the peace of mind.

While you're at the hardware store, get a few extra copies of your new key made, and give one to a trusted friend, neighbor, or relative for emergencies.

6. Find out where your shut-off valves are.

One of your first lines of defense when it comes to common homeowner emergencies or preventing major damage due to burst water pipes for example— is knowing where the shut-off valves are. Being able to turn off the water (or gas, or electricity) quickly is vital to minimizing damages.

First, there are shut-off valves for small, localized problems: If the toilet is overflowing, look for the valve coming out of the floor or the wall behind the toilet and turn that to the right to stop the water flow. If your sink or faucet is leaking uncontrollably, the shut-offs will usually be under the sink (one for cold and one for hot).

Likewise, there should be a gas shut-off valve near your stove or dryer if either one uses natural gas. Find and familiarize yourself with all of these local shut-offs.

Then — and most importantly — find your *main* shut-offs, which control the gas and water coming into your house from the street. They're usually found in the basement, toward the front of your house, but not always. Learn where these are ahead of time so you're not clumsily searching for them in a panic as a geyser of a busted pipe is gushing water all over your kitchen.

Your circuit breaker acts as a shut-off for your home's electricity. Individual circuits will control the electric flow to certain rooms or appliances — one breaker switch might shut off all the overhead lights, while another might control the refrigerator and the microwave outlets. Get familiar with the circuit breaker, and note where the main shut-off switch is to turn off all power in an emergency (if water is leaking into a live light fixture, for instance).

7. Plan now for emergencies.

The time to be researching plumbers in your area is not when the toilet is broken and spewing sewage onto the bathroom floor.

Ask your new neighbors for the names of anyone that they'd recommend, including plumbers, electricians, and handymen.

Also, look up the numbers for poison control and local emergency services (if it's not just 911) and put them on the fridge. Check all your smoke detectors and replace the batteries if you need to — you can also ask the fire department to come by and inspect them. Finally, find all of your emergency exits, and make a family fire plan that also designates a meeting point outside.

8. Use your home inspection report to plan future upgrades.

Your home inspector should give you a comprehensive report indicating the condition of all the major systems and structural parts of your home. This information can form the basis of your long-term home improvement game plan.

From there, make some lists: The stuff that was fairly easy to accomplish — or simply critical can go on the short-term, right-away list. The items that are not as important may have to wait.

9. Get a small safe or filing cabinet.

Even if you've never had one before, you're probably going to need a filing cabinet and/or small safe. File your closing statement and all the paperwork from your home purchase in the filing cabinet and put the important documents in the safe.

And that's just the beginning of a lot of paperwork you'll be filing from here on out. Keep receipts and instruction manuals for any new appliances you buy, your insurance and property tax bills, and any estimates or receipts from contractors as you make improvements.

10. Create a seasonal home maintenance checklist, and start using it.

There are some maintenance tasks you'll have to do to your home annually or semi-annually to keep it in good shape. And depending on the season you move in, it's probably time to get started on some of them.

This checklist is broken down into spring and fall:

Spring/early summer home maintenance checklist

- **Test your smoke detectors:** Fire safety professionals recommend doing this whenever the clocks spring ahead or fall back. Change any dead batteries.
- **Clean your gutters**: Leaves and other debris from fall and winter may have choked up the gutters, and you will want them free and clear before April's heavy rains. If you have a one-story house, this is easy to do yourself; if your home is two or more stories or you're afraid of heights, it should only cost about $60-$100 to have a pro come and do it.
- **Fertilize or plant new grass**: The time to plant and fertilize grass is early spring: With the nights still cold, grass grows but weeds don't. If you get a nice thick lawn growing by May, it can naturally crowd out the more unsavory stuff like crabgrass and dandelions. (If you don't mind some chemicals, you can use crabgrass preventer or weed-blocking fertilizer — but usually not with new grass seed.)
- **Clean out your dryer vent**: Your lint screen may be full. Clean it out with a vacuum or a long, bendy brush once a year to improve your dryer's efficiency.
- **Install window A/C units (or check central air units)**: The time to lug these things down from the attic and wrestle them into place is *before* the first scorching hot day, not right in the middle of it. Clean the filters before firing them up for the season.
- **Clean ceiling fans**: They can get pretty dusty up there sitting idle all winter long.
- **Stain or paint the deck**: Every other year or so, you'll need to add another coat of stain to your deck's floorboards (the railings and spindles can usually go five years or more). On a dry spring day, give it a good cleaning, and then strap a roller brush to a broom handle and slap another coat on there to protect the wood.

Fall/early winter home maintenance checklist:

- **Chimney sweep**: You should get your main boiler or furnace chimney swept every couple of years—buildup in there can cause a chimney fire. And if you have a wood-burning fireplace or wood stove, get that cleaned out every couple of years or every time you go through a cord of wood, whichever comes first.
- **Boiler/furnace clean-out**: Before heating season begins, you should get an inspection and the recommended annual maintenance on your boiler or furnace. If you get oil delivery, your oil company should take care of this for you. With gas, you'll need to call your own plumber or heating technician.

- **Store hoses and turn off the water to outside spigots**: You don't want water freezing in there and breaking the pipes. In the basement, just follow the pipe from the faucet to the nearest shut-off valve, and turn it clockwise or so it's perpendicular to the pipe.

- **Secure items**: Move patio furniture into the garage (or at least take the cushions inside), cover up the grill, and remove and store your window A/C units (or cover up your central air unit). Move snow shovels, and other snow gear to an accessible spot in the garage or shed.

- **Tune up your snow blower**: Snow blowers take a beating each winter — the metal parts get soaked, they get road salt inside them… it's easy for them to get rust and stop working. Take care of this because you will want yours ready to perform when that first foot of snow falls.

11. Go Shopping

Unless you're downsizing, you might need some new home furnishings to fill out your new place. Maybe you're moving from a small kitchenette to a large eat-in kitchen, or your old couch was too big or too ratty to move. Whatever the case, you may need to fill some empty rooms.

12. Throw a housewarming party.

Your first few weeks in a new house are going to be filled with the adrenaline and excitement that comes with such a big life change.

For most people, whatever isn't unpacked after about two months just stays in boxes and gets shoved in a closet. If you haven't put pictures up on the wall after a couple of months, you're going to be looking at empty walls for a long time.

Throwing a housewarming party is a great idea after you move in to your new home. It gives you a defined deadline to get the place in order, and puts just the right amount of motivational pressure on you to keep at it.

It will allow you to share your excitement and hard work with the people you care about—not to mention, you might get a nice gift or two.

Realize that you will make many more improvements to your home—it does not have to be done all at one time.

19 Ways to Immediately Save Money

So you've just moved into your new home. You've unloaded the boxes and started to unpack your life.Right now is the *perfect* time to walk through a checklist of ways to save money on your home for years to come.

Starting on these things as early as possible will allow you to start saving money sooner rather than later. Plus, some of them will be easier to accomplish before you hang pictures or get too settled in and lose your move-in momentum.

Here are 19 things to check or do immediately that will reduce the energy and maintenance costs of your home over the long haul.

1. Check the insulation in your attic—and install more if needed.

   If you have an unfinished attic, pop your head up there and take a look around. You should see insulation up there between the beams, and there should be at least six inches of it everywhere (more if you live in the northern part of the United States).

   If there's inadequate insulation up there—or the insulation you have appears to be damaged—install new insulation.

2. Lower the temperature on your hot water heater down to 120 degrees Fahrenheit (55 degrees Celsius).

   This is the optimum temperature for your hot water heater. Most people don't use water hotter than 120 degrees — indeed, water hotter than that can scald you or a child — and thus the energy needed to keep the water above 120 degrees isn't used effectively. Lower the temperature to save money on your energy bill.

3. Toss a water heater blanket over that hot water heater as well.

   While most modern hot water heaters are well-insulated, some are insulated better than others, and many older heaters aren't insulated well at all. A small investment in a blanket for your water heater will slowly and gradually save you money on your heating bill over time by keeping the heat in the water instead of letting it disperse slowly into your basement or utility closet.

4. Install ceiling fans in most rooms.

   Ceiling fans are a low-energy way to keep air moving in your home. Because of the air circulation effect, you can get away with keeping your thermostat a degree or two higher in summer and a degree or two lower in winter, netting a rather large savings.

   The most important thing to know is that the air directly below the fan should be blowing *down* on you in the summer and should be pulled upwards away from you in the winter — you can use the reversal switch on your fan to switch between the modes at the start of each season.

5. Wrap exposed water pipes with insulation.

   Exposed hot water pipes lose heat as they move water from your heater to your faucet or shower. Wrapping them in pipe insulation, especially in cold basements or garages, can make a two- to four-degree difference in the temperature of the water, and also allows hot water to reach your faucet faster.

   Check the pipes into and out of your hot water heater first, as the first three feet out of the heater (and the last few feet of inlet water) are key. Use good-quality pipe insulation for the job.

6. Install a programmable thermostat—and learn how to use it.

   A programmable thermostat allows you to schedule automatic increases and decreases in your home's temperature, saving money on cooling in the summer and heating in the winter.

They're easy to install and easy to use, especially if you keep a fairly routine schedule. Just program the thermostat to drop a few degrees at night while you're sleeping or off at work during the day, and set it to return to your preferred temperature just before you wake up or return home from work. You won't notice the difference and you will see a lower utility bill.

7. Replace your air filters.

   When you first move in, you almost always need to replace the air handling filter or the filter on your furnace or AC unit. Don't worry, it's easy to do—it takes about 10 seconds.

   Go down to your air handling unit, find where the filter is (it's almost always a large rectangle), and mark down the measurements (printed around the edges). Then, go to the hardware store and pick up a few of them. Go home and replace the old one with a new filter, and save the rest so you always have a clean one ready to go. An outdated filter not only doesn't filter air as well, it also has a negative impact on air flow, meaning your air handling system or HVAC unit has to work harder — and use more energy — to pump out lower quality air.

8. Make sure the vents in all rooms are clear of dust and obstructions.

   None of the vents in your home should be covered or blocked by anything—doing that makes your heating and cooling work overtime. You should also look into all of your vents and make sure they're as dust-free as possible, and brush them out if you see any dust bunnies. This improves air flow into the room, reducing the amount of blowing that needs to happen.

9. Mark any cracks in the basement with dated masking tape.

   Many homes have a few small cracks in their basement walls from the settling of the foundation and the weight of the house. In a stable home, the small cracks aren't growing at all—they're safe. If they're growing, however, you'll save a *ton* of money by getting the problem addressed *now* rather than later.

   How do you tell if they're growing? Take some masking tape and cover up the end of any cracks you notice inside or outside, and write today's date on the tape. Then, in a few months, check the tape–if you see a crack growing out of the end of the tape, you might have a problem and should call a specialist before the problem gets out of hand.

10. Hang a clothes rack in your laundry room (or better yet, an outdoor clothesline).

    Even an efficient clothes dryer can really eat up your energy costs, but it's convenient for many people. If you're willing to battle that convenience, you can save money by hanging a clothes rack from the wall in the laundry room and using it for some items; t-shirts, underwear, towels, and pillow cases dry great on clothes racks. If you can hang up 20% of the clothes in a load on a rack, you can get away with running the dryer 20% less than before, saving you cash.

    Even better: If you can, install a clothesline in your back yard and hang most of your clothes to dry outside, where a good breeze can do the work of a dryer in no time — and at no cost.

11. Check all toilets and under-sink plumbing for leaks or constant running & check faucets, too.

    Do surveys of the plumbing in your home before you settle in. If you find a toilet is running constantly, it's going to cost you money so fix that constantly running toilet. You should also peek under the basin of all the sinks in your home, just to make sure there aren't any leaks. Got a leaky faucet? You should repair or replace any of those, because the drip-drip-drip of water is also a drip-drip-drip of money; not to mention the terrible interplay between mold and home insurance.

12. Install LED or CFL light bulbs.

    LED and CFL bulbs can save you a lot of money on energy use over the long haul, plus they have much longer lives than normal incandescent bulbs, making them well worth the upfront investment. Consider installing some in various places — especially in areas where the lights may be in use for long periods, like the living room or kitchen, or left on accidentally, like a back hallway or basement. CFL bulbs tend to be cheaper, but LED bulbs are usually preferable in terms of performance, and have come down in cost quite a bit over the past few years.

13. Choose energy efficient appliances, even if you have to pay more up front.

    Unless you were lucky enough to buy a fully-furnished home, you'll likely have to do some appliance shopping. Focus on reliability and energy efficiency above all, even if that seriously increases the cost you have to pay up front. A refrigerator that uses little energy and lasts 20 years is far, far cheaper over the long run than a fridge that runs for seven years and guzzles electricity. If you plan ahead, you can buy it with a credit card that offers a big sign-up bonus. You'll pay the balance off immediately and walk away with hundreds in cash or travel rewards.

14. Set up your home electronics with a SmartStrip or two.

    Looking forward to getting your television, cable box, DVD player, sound system, and video game console set up? When you do it, set things up with proper surge protection (to shield your equipment from electric surges). You might also want to consider a SmartStrip, which makes it easy to "unplug" devices that aren't in use.

    A SmartStrip allows the on-off status of one device — say, the television — to control whether or not there's power flowing to other devices (say, the DVD player or the video game console). Having the power cut automatically from such auxiliary devices can save a lot of money over time, especially since many such devices eat quite a bit of power as they sit there in standby mode, constantly draining your money.

15. Plant shade trees near your house.

    Mother nature can help you save significantly on your summer cooling costs — and heating costs in winter, too.

Plant deciduous trees — the kind that lose their leaves in the fall — on the western and eastern sides of your house. The leafy shade trees will naturally cool your home during the hot summer months by reducing the amount of direct sunlight that hits your house.

In the winter, they'll lose their leaves, allowing that same sunlight to stream through your windows and heat up the home a bit more. And if you plant evergreens on the north and northwest sides of your home, they won't affect the sunlight, but will shield your home from cold winter winds.

As an added benefit, mature trees can increase your property value. Just make sure to plant them a safe distance from power lines and your home itself (no one wants a downed limb poking through their roof). Plant them now, and they'll grow and shade your house sooner.

16. Change the locks and make spare keys.

One of the first things many homeowners do is change the locks on their new home. You don't need to be particularly handy to install new door hardware, and a set of basic doorknobs and locks for your front and back door will only set you back $20-$80 or so. It may seem unnecessary, but there's no way to know whether there are copies of your old key floating around. Investing a bit of money and time today can protect you from burglary down the road.

Also get an extra copy of your key made and leave it with someone you trust, so you don't have to shell out $100 to a locksmith when you inevitably lock yourself out.

17. Air-seal your home.

This isn't such a problem in new homes but in older homes. It's important to look for any places where air may be leaking directly into or out of your home. Common trouble spots are around doorways, windows, and even electric outlets.

18. Take advantage of tax benefits and other incentives.

The energy tax credit, which was set to expire in 2014, was renewed at the last minute in December. That means homeowners who made energy-based improvements to their homes last year were eligible to receive a tax credit for 10% of the cost, up to $500 lifetime. Whether this popular credit is renewed for another year, however, is anyone's guess. A whopping 30% tax credit toward the cost of solar energy systems, residential wind turbines, and geothermal heat pumps is in effect through 2016.

Your state or city may offer even more benefits, from no-interest loans to rebates, so do some research when you invest money improving the efficiency of your home — you may save even more money than you expected.

Many states and local utility companies also provide home energy audits for free or at a discount. Someone will thoroughly inspect your home to find where you're wasting energy. They'll look for air leaks and un-insulated pipes, test the efficiency of your heating and cooling equipment, and even replace any older incandescent light bulbs for free.

19. Create a home maintenance checklist, and run through it for the first time.

    This list should include regular home maintenance tasks that you'd want to do on a monthly, quarterly, or annual basis. Then, make it a habit to run through the items on this list every so often. Doing so will extend the life of almost everything in your home, saving you buckets of money over time.

123's of moving in

1. Inspect Delivered Boxes

   You do have the household inventory you prepared or received during the moving preparations, right? Check each moving box against the detailed list as it is carried inside your new home, and if a box or a household item happens to be missing, notify the moving crew right away and check together if it was left in the moving truck by mistake.

   Once the movers leave, inspect each moving container for visual damage or any other signs of obvious mistreatment. If you find broken or damaged goods, note down the specific damage in your inventory list and contact the moving company in an attempt to resolve the issue peacefully. If you were prudent enough to choose reliable and trustworthy movers, the dispute should be resolved quickly in your favor. However, should the moving company decide to play dumb, exercise your consumer rights and file a complaint against your movers.

2. Get Your Utilities Up and Running

   You should have arranged the connection of the main house utilities before the move, but if you haven't done it for one reason or another, do so without delay. Naturally, the first utility companies to call are the power and water providers—things will look much brighter and smoother once you have electricity, gas and running water in your new house.

   Having taken care of the fundamental utilities, consider making the necessary arrangements to gain access to the Internet, phone, and other important services.

3. 3. Unpack Essentials

   Proceed by unpacking your essential boxes and prepare the two most important rooms for normal use—the bedroom and bathroom. Moving days have the tendency to drain out people's energy so you'll definitely need a place to lay your weary body at the end of the most stressful day when moving. Assemble your bed (if necessary), unpack the box labeled as "Bedding" and prepare your bed for sweet dreams. Before you call it a day, however, you'll desperately need to take a refreshing shower, so dig into the "Bathroom" container and take out the shower curtains, the towels, your favorite bathrobe, plus all the toiletries you'll need to take away the stress and dirt of moving day.

   Of course, unpacking and arranging the kitchen is also a priority but the task can wait a few days until you get back on your feet.

4. Get Organized

It's very important that you find the time to prioritize your post-move time. Take out a notebook and start writing down all the immediate tasks that you'll have to take care of in the next few days, and even weeks. Just like the moving calendar enabled you to have a stress- and trouble-free move, this prioritized to-do list will clearly jump-start the speedy process of settling in your new home and your smooth period of acclimatization to the unknown surroundings.

5. Inspect Your House Thoroughly

One of the first things to do after moving into a new house is to get to know your place inside out. Locate your favorite magnifying glass and inspect every nook and cranny of your new home as meticulously and passionately as if your birth name were Sherlock Holmes.

Inspect each and every room for visible signs of damage, especially from water or fire. Check for plumbing leaks, dripping faucets, and running toilets. One clever trick to make sure there are no water leaks of any kind is to register the readings of your water meter at the start and end of a period of several hours when no water is used anywhere in the house. If the two readings differ, then it's a sure sign that you have a leaking problem and you'll need to localize and fix it (or have it fixed).

Moreover, scour the front yard, the backyard and the perimeter of your house for any troublesome problems and do what's necessary to eliminate them.

6. Locate Fuse Box and Main Water Valve

Make sure you know where your circuit breaker box and main water valve are located in case of emergencies, or just in case you're about to fix a power or water issue and need to turn off the electricity or cut off the water supply.

You must know which fuse controls which part of your new house if the fuses are not labeled at all or if the guy before you got it all wrong. Identify and label each circuit breaker accordingly. Similarly, get familiar with how the main water stop valve works and see if it functions properly by checking for any running water after the valve has been turned off. Replace it, or get it replaced if it's not working the way it should.

7. Secure Your New Home

Once the utilities have been connected, the house has been inspected for problems and the emergency centers located, it's time to secure your new home against unauthorized access or harmful acts of nature.

Change the locks on all outside doors to ensure that you and your family are the only persons who have access to your new home. Double-check all windows and doors and make sure they close securely. Install smoke detectors in every room. Provide at least one functional fire-extinguisher per floor. Purchase a few first-aid kits. Devise an escape plan out of the house in case of emergencies and make it known to each family member. Consult specialists and consider installing a burglar alarm, especially if your home is situated in a neighborhood with a relatively bad reputation.

8. Childproof Your New Home

If you just moved into a new home with a baby or toddler, your house will have to go one step beyond the usual household security, and this additional step is called childproofing. Also known as baby-proofing, this safety step is more like a series of steps—an entire process which includes timely identification of all household hazards that can await your little child.

Start the childproofing process from the room your baby or toddler will be spending most of their time—the nursery room. Leave only two items in the crib—your happy baby and the fitted mattress sheet. Secure the changing table against accidental tip-over's, mount window guards and cordless blinds on the windows and electric outlet protectors on the walls.

Make your way to the bathroom and take all precautionary measures so that the bathing time of your little angel is nothing but fun. The kitchen, the stairs, and the living room are the other premises in your new house where things could go very wrong for your baby or toddler.

9. Connect Major Appliances

If you have chosen to move your fridge, freezer, washing machine or dishwasher instead of selling them, giving them away to friends, donating them to charity or just throwing them away now is the time to connect them and thus finish the process of unpacking and setting up the most delicious room in your new house—the kitchen.

Refrigerators are the most fragile appliances from the ones mentioned above and extra care should be taken in their preparation and actual relocation. Just like millions of other people, you're probably very interested in knowing the answer to the question, "How long do you have to let a fridge sit after moving it?" You need to leave your fridge upright on its final kitchen spot for at least 3 full hours before you can plug it in and turn it on after moving. This is roughly the time it takes for the oil, which must have escaped the compressor and flown into the cooling lines, to return to the heart of the cooling mechanism—the compressor.

10. Continue Unpacking

You already unpacked the essentials boxes and furnished and arranged the most frequently used rooms, but what about the rest of your new residence? Step by step, the unpacking process will stretch out and reach the living room, spare guest room, garage, basement, attic and every other storage areas of your home.

If you rate your unpacking pace as "excruciatingly slow" and you wish all items had been unpacked by now, you have a couple of options to speed up that slow post-move stage. You can either dig deeper into your pockets or hire a professional unpacking team to get the job done in no time, or you can organize an unpacking party and invite good friends to help you out in exchange for refreshing drinks, tasty food and your eternal gratitude.

11. Recycle Packing Materials

Unpacking will leave you with plenty of packing materials which you may no longer need. Of course, a number of the moving boxes you used during the relocation will be in such a bad shape that you will have no other option but to throw them away for recycling. Others, however, will be good enough to survive the stress of another move and those you can keep for yourself or give to friends in need.

12. Clean Your House

Without a doubt, unpacking will also leave you with tons of garbage, dust, and dirt.

Purchase quality cleaning products and turn your new house into a fresh and welcoming home. Everything should be dust-free, polished and shiny: carpets—vacuum floors—mopped, reflective surfaces—spotless, furniture pieces—gleaming and neatly arranged.

If you feel that you won't be able to spare the time or you know that your budget can easily take you off the hook, consider hiring professional cleaning services to give your new house the refreshed look it deserves.

13. Tend To Your Pet's Needs

Cleaning your place will also give you a peace of mind if you have a pet. Dogs and cats have a developed sense of smell and can usually sniff out traces of other pets who may have lived in the house before and cause them to start marking their territory. The territorial issue aside, your pet will probably have additional troubles getting used to the strange environment.

Your dog or cat may become a victim of separation anxiety. Just monitor your pet closely if they seem depressed, refuse to eat or exhibit unusual behavior after a move. Keep your cat indoors for the first few days, ideally confined to a single room but provide all the comforts they are used to having, including a number of items from their old life to keep them calm. Introduce your home to your pet slowly, only one room at a time until they get accustomed to the unfamiliar sounds, sights, and smells. As far as your dog goes, take them on short leashed walks to green areas around the neighborhood for a quicker adaptation.

14. Change Your Address

If you failed to register your current address with the post office online, then you should do it now. Also now is the perfect opportunity to inform your friends and specific institutions of your changed postal address. Of course, you should also contact banks, credit card companies, insurance companies and other important institutions and inform them of your recent change of address.

If you've changed cities, don't forget to update your information on the voter's registration for your local area.

15. Find A Good School For Your Child

You might have taken care of this task way before the actual move, but then again, you may have just forgotten to do it. If you moved to a new city, you need to find a good school and register your school-age child as soon as possible.

Armed with your kid's school records, a good way to start the search is to go online (for example, visit the webpage of the National Center for Education Statistics) and look for suitable educational institutions for your child. Another sensible way to approach the situation is to ask your coworkers and neighbors for advice in the form of recommendations. Whichever method you prefer to explore, visit the shortlisted schools together with your kid to get a feel for the academic environment. It's a good idea to call the schools beforehand and arrange a meeting with the principal and/or some of the senior teachers there.

16. Find Health Care Providers

One of the most important things you need to do when moving into a new house in a new city is to find the right health care providers for you and your family. In reality, the task is more than important.

If you have good recommendations from your previous health care provider, then you have nothing to worry about. But if you don't, you'll have to find a doctor who is right for you, for your children and for your pets. Similar to the process of finding a good school, the hunt for a trustworthy primary care doctor, a dentist or a vet should either begin online or even better—through specific suggestions and recommendations from your colleagues at work or the folks who live next door. Take into account your specific medical needs, the doctor's experience and personality and don't make your final decision before visiting the office in person and having a little chat with your future physician.

17. Register Your Vehicle

Moving into a new home in a new state means that you're going to have to register your motor vehicle in the new state and then transfer your driver's license. In order to cross this task as completed, visit your local DMV office in person and take care of this formality before the deadline is reached (some states give a window of 10 days to register your car while others give as many as 30 days).

At the DMV office, be ready to present a proof of insurance as you are required to purchase insurance from the state you just relocated to.

18. Assess Your Financial and Insurance Situation

Once the relocation is over, it's important that you sit down and assess your current financial situation. Did the move go over your allocated moving budget or did you manage to fit it in?

If you just moved to a new state, you'll probably need to set up new bank accounts as well. Also, contact your insurance companies and check whether you're still covered at your new home or you'll need to create new insurance policies (household, auto, health, etc.) with a different insurer.

19. Set up Your Home to Your Flawless Taste

Moving into a new home gives you a great opportunity to arrange and decorate your house exactly the way you've always wanted. Now is the perfect time to let out the masterful interior designer in you.

You are free to purchase new furniture pieces and decorative items, you can play with various colors and shapes, you're encouraged to experiment with different home décor techniques in order to create a peaceful, relaxing and beautiful atmosphere in your home. Add a reasonable number of soft lighting sources throughout your residence to emphasize its charm and place pretty vases of refreshing flowers on specific spots to double the positive energy flow in your living space.

20. Greet Your New Neighbors

Everybody needs a bit of guidance when placed in a completely unfamiliar environment. New house, new neighborhood, new city, new state—it'll take some time before this strange sense of unfamiliarity goes away. And until then, it's the exciting prospect of making new friends to get you through the acclimatization process quickly and smoothly.

Even before you're done unpacking, consider going over to your neighbors next door and introduce yourself. This initial introduction is not only a sign of good manners, but it's also a chance for you to befriend local people who will undoubtedly help you learn your ways around your new living area.

21. Check for Plumbing Leaks

Your home inspector should have done this for you before closing, but it never hurts to double-check. Keep an eye out for dripping faucets and running toilets, and check your water heater for signs of a leak. Check your water meter at the beginning and end of a two-hour window in which no water is being used in your house. If the reading is different, you have a leak.

22. Steam Clean Carpets

Do this before you move your furniture in, and your new home life will be off to a fresh start. You can pay a professional carpet cleaning service — you'll pay about $50 per room; most services require a minimum of about $100 before they'll come out — or you can rent a steam cleaner for about $30 per day and do the work yourself.

23. Wipe out Your Cabinets

Thoroughly wipe down your cabinets before you move in your dishes and bathroom supplies. Make sure to wipe inside and out, preferably with a non-toxic cleaner, and replace contact paper if necessary.

24. Give Critters the Heave-Ho

That includes mice, rats, bats, termites, roaches, and any other uninvited guests. There are any number of DIY ways to get rid of pests, but if you need to bring out the big guns, an initial visit from a pest removal service will run you $100 to $300, followed by monthly or quarterly visits at about $50 each time.

25. Introduce Yourself to Your Circuit Breaker Box and Main Water Valve

It's a good idea to figure out which fuses control what parts of your house and label them accordingly. This will take two people: One to stand in the room where the power is supposed to go off, the other to trip the fuses and yell, "Did that work? How about now?"

You'll want to know how to turn off your main water valve if you have a plumbing emergency, if a hurricane or tornado is headed your way, or if you're going out of town. Just locate the valve — it could be inside or outside your house — and turn the knob until it's off. Test it by turning on any faucet in the house; no water should come out.

26. Make a Prioritized List

The minute you walk in to your new home, your mind will be racing with to-dos. Keep this overwhelming task list at bay by keeping a notebook in a central location and write down every action item you or your family thinks of throughout the day. After 24 hours cut the list off, and prioritize each item with a 1, 2, or 3. First priority should be items completed that week - such as safety concerns, cleaning, unpacking essentials, etc. Priority two should be tasks completed within the next two months - related to organization, maintenance and remaining unpacking. Priority three tasks should be non-essentials, but improvements and projects you'd like to complete within the year - renovations, landscaping, and large purchases.

27. Clean Refrigerator Coils or Pay Unnecessary Repair Bills

Refrigerator condenser coils are located on the back of the fridge or across the bottom. When coils are clogged with dust, pet hair and cobwebs, they can't efficiently release heat. The result is your compressor works harder and longer than it was designed to, using more energy and shortening the life of your fridge. Clean the coils with a coil-cleaning brush and vacuum. A coil-cleaning brush, which is bendable to fit in tight areas, does a thorough job. Look for one online or at appliance stores.

28. Clean Out the Lint for Dryer Efficiency and Save up to $25 a Year

A clogged lint screen or dryer duct drastically reduces the efficiency of your dryer, whether it's gas or electric. Clean the lint screen after each load and clean the exhaust duct once a year. Electric dryers use about $85 of electricity annually. A dirty lint screen can cause the dryer to use up to 30 percent more electricity, according to the Consumer Energy Center. Lint buildup is also a common cause of fires.

Dry loads of laundry back-to-back so the dryer doesn't cool down between loads (a warm dryer uses less energy). And only run the dryer until the clothes are dry. Overdrying damages your clothes and runs up your electric bill. If you're in the market for a new dryer and already have a gas line in the house, go with a gas dryer. A gas dryer is more efficient.

29. Install a Detachable Toilet Seat

It seems like no matter how hard you try, you can never get the hinges on the toilet seat clean. There's always a bit of cleaning solution that seeps underneath and creeps out later. Installing a detachable toilet seat solves the problem. This Bemis brand seat is easy to remove by just twisting two hinge caps about a quarter of a turn. Then you have easy access to clean under the hinges. Detachable seats cost about $20. Installation is straightforward and only requires a wrench.

30. Replace the furnace filter.

One of the fastest ways to create problems with a forced-air heating and cooling system is to forget to replace the filter. Locate the furnace filter and buy replacements if the previous owners didn't leave you a stash. Replace the filter (and get in the habit of doing it every month).

31. Clean Air Conditioner Condensers and Evaporators

A little sweat equity now will help both your wallet and your comfort level later when summer's heat sets in. Most of the job can be done without the help of a professional, and by servicing and testing out your cooling system now, you will have plenty of time to make an appointment with an air conditioning contractor if there's any unforeseen issues. After cutting off the electricity to the unit, vacuum the outdoor condenser's exterior fins with a soft-bristled brush, and clear away bushes, weeds and overgrown grass within two feet of the unit. Indoors, replace the furnace filter on the evaporator unit, vacuum the blower compartment, and clean the condensation drain.

32. Locate your home's main water shutoff valve.

Know where you main water shutoff valve is in case you need to shut off the water to your entire house.

Almost all homes have one main shutoff valve directly before the water meter and another directly after. Where the meter is located depends on the climate in your area. In cold climates, the meter and main shutoff valves are located inside, usually in a basement or other warm area to prevent freezing. In milder climates, the meter and its two shutoff valves may be attached to an exterior wall or nestled in an underground box with a removable lid.

Between the water main in the street and the meter, there's also usually a buried *curb stop valve* (accessible only by city workers wielding special long-handled wrenches) and a *corporation stop*, where your house water line hooks up to the water main. Your city absolutely doesn't want you messing around with these valves. Turn your water off or on using the main valve on the *house side* of the meter. This valve will normally be a gate-type valve, with a round knurled handle, requiring several full clockwise rotations to turn off. In newer homes, it could be a ball valve.

33. Locate the electrical panel.

Find the electrical panel so you know where to shut of the power to your whole house or an individual circuit.

You'll usually find the main circuit breaker panel—a gray, metal box—in a utility room, garage or basement. Don't worry about opening the panel's door. All the dangerous stuff is behind another steel cover. Behind the door is the main breaker for the entire house (usually at the top of the panel) and two rows of other breakers below it, each controlling individual circuits. If you're lucky, there will be a guide that indicates which outlets and receptacles are served by each circuit.

34. Inspect crawlspaces and the attic.

It's good to familiarize yourself with the farthest corners of your home. Check for leaks, bugs, mold and other issues that you should address sooner rather than later. If your crawlspace doesn't have a vapor barrier, learn how to install one.

35. Check smoke and CO detector dates and replace, as needed.

It's important that you know where your smoke and CO detectors are located and that you make sure they are working. Smoke alarms may be the cheapest, easiest and most effective means for protecting your family and your home from a fire, as long as they're functioning. Learn where smoke detectors should be located, how to maintain them, when to replace them.

36. If you don't have keyless entry, hide a key.

If you don't have keyless locks, be sure to hide a house key so you don't get locked out. Consider a location other than under the welcome mat, like in a garden hose or under a flower pot.

37. Add Inexpensive Door and Window Alarms

Keeping doors and windows locked is your first line of defense. Make wireless alarms your second. Burglars hate noises, so even a small alarm usually sends them running. The alarms are available at home centers. Or check out Intermatic or Door and Window Alarms. The alarms don't provide the same security as pro-installed monitored systems since the wireless devices are activated by doors or windows opening (not glass breaking). Use the alarms for doors and windows in 'hidden' areas of the house where you don't normally gather and that are often dark.

Attach the alarm to the door or window (with a screw or double-sided tape) alongside the magnetic contact strip (they don't have to be touching, but within 1/2 in.). When the door or window opens, breaking magnetic contact, the alarm shrieks (these little units have a piercing alarm). The door alarm has a delay feature, giving you time to set the alarm and leave, then open the door and deactivate the unit when you come home, without setting it off. The window unit has an on/off switch. The alarms will work on any door or window, and the batteries last two to three years.

New Homeowner Summary Checklist

________ Take a few days off
________ Do improvements/repairs before you move in
________ Change your address/set up utilities
________ Clean
________ Change locks
________ Find shut off valves
________ Plan for emergencies
________ Use home inspection report
________ Get a small safe
________ Create a home maintenance checklist
________ Go shopping
________ Throw a housewarming party

19 Ways to save money Summary Checklist

________ Check the insulation
________ Lower temperature on hot water heater
________ Toss a blanket on your water heater
________ Install ceiling fans
________ Wrap exposed Water pipes with insulation
________ Install a programmable thermostat
________ Replace your filters
________ Make sure vents in all rooms are clear of obstructions
________ Mark any cracks in the basement
________ Hang clothes in your laundry room
________ Check all toilets under sink plumbing for leaks
________ Install LED or CFL lights

- ________ Choose energy efficient appliances
- ________ Set up your home electronics with a smart strip
- ________ Plant shade trees
- ________ Change the locks
- ________ Air seal your home
- ________ Take advantage of tax benefits
- ________ Create a home maintenance checklist

123's of moving in Summary Checklist

- ________ Inspect delivered boxes
- ________ Get your utilities up and running
- ________ Unpack essentials
- ________ Get organized
- ________ Inspect your house thoroughly
- ________ Locate your fuse box and main water valve
- ________ Secure your new home
- ________ Childproof your new house
- ________ Connect major appliances
- ________ Continue unpacking
- ________ Recycle packing materials
- ________ Clean your house
- ________ Tend to your pets
- ________ Change your address
- ________ Find a good school for your children
- ________ Find health care providers
- ________ Register your vehicle
- ________ Assess your financial insurance
- ________ Set up your home to your taste
- ________ Greet your new neighbors
- ________ Check for plumbing leaks

________ Steam clean carpets
________ Wipe out your cabinets
________ Drive out critters
________ Introduce yourself to your circuit breaker box
________ Make a prioritized list
________ Clean refrigerator coils
________ Clean out lint for dryer efficiency
________ Install a detachable toilet seat
________ Replace the furnace filter
________ Clean air conditioner condensers
________ Locate your homes main water shutoff valve
________ Locate the electrical panel
________ Inspect crawlspace and attic
________ Check smoke and Co detectors
________ Keyless entry/ hide a key
________ Add inexpensive door and window alarms

TASKS OF YOUR REALTOR—WHAT DO THEY REALLY DO?

CHAPTER

6

In this chapter:

Pre-Listing Activities

Listing Property Appointment

After Listing Agreement is Signed

Entering Property in MLS Databse

Marketing the Listing

The Offer and the Contract

Tracking the Loan

Home Inspection

The Appraisal

Closing Preparations and Duties

Follow Up After Closing

Most clients are not aware of all the services that agents provide to sellers and buyers during the course of the transaction, probably because most of the important services are performed behind the scenes. Here is a detailed list of what you can expect from your Real Estate Agent.

Pre-Listing Activities

1. Make appointment with seller for listing presentation.
2. Send a written or e-mail confirmation of appointment and call to confirm.
3. Review appointment questions.
4. Research all comparable currently listed properties.
5. Research sales activity for past 18 months from MLS and public databases.
6. Research "average days on market" for properties similar in type, price and location.
7. Download and review property tax roll information.
8. Prepare "comparable market analysis" (CMA) to establish market value.
9. Obtain copy of subdivision plat/complex layout.
10. Research property's ownership and deed type.
11. Research property's public record information for lot size and dimensions.
12. Verify legal description.
13. Research property's land use coding and deed restrictions.
14. Research property's current use and zoning.
15. Verify legal names of owner(s) in county's public property records.
16. Prepare listing presentation package with above materials.
17. Perform exterior "curb appeal assessment" of subject property.

18. Compile and assemble formal file on property.
19. Confirm current public schools and explain their impact on market value.
20. Review listing appointment checklist to ensure completion of all tasks.

Listing Appointment Presentation

21. Give seller an overview of current market conditions and projections.
22. Review agent and company credentials and accomplishments.
23. Present company's profile and position or "niche" in the marketplace.
24. Present CMA results, including comparables, solds, current listings and expireds.
25. Offer professional pricing strategy based and interpretation of current market conditions.
26. Discuss goals to market effectively.
27. Explain market power and benefits of multiple listing service.
28. Explain market power of Web marketing, IDX and REALTOR.com.
29. Explain the work the broker and agent do "behind the scenes" and agent's availability.
30. Explain agent's role in screening qualified buyers to protect against curiosity seekers.
31. Present and discuss strategic master marketing plan.
32. Explain different agency relationships and determine seller's preference.
33. Review all clauses in listing contract and obtain seller's signature.

After Listing Agreement is Signed

34. Review current title information.
35. Measure overall and heated square footage.
36. Measure interior room sizes.
37. Confirm lot size via owner's copy of certified survey, if available.
38. Note any and all unrecorded property lines, agreements, easements.
39. Obtain house plans, if applicable and available.
40. Review house plans, make copy.
41. Order plat map for retention in property's listing file.
42. Prepare showing instructions for buyers' agents and agree on showing time with seller.
43. Obtain current mortgage loan(s) information: companies and account numbers.

44. Verify current loan information with lender(s).
45. Check assumability of loan(s) and any special requirements.
46. Discuss possible buyer financing alternatives and options with seller.
47. Review current appraisal if available.
48. Identify Home Owner Association manager is applicable.
49. Verify Home Owner Association fees and current annual fee.
50. Order copy of Home Owner Association bylaws, if applicable.
51. Research electricity availability and supplier's name and phone number.
52. Calculate average utility usage from last 12 months of bills.
53. Research and verify city sewer/septic tank system.
54. Calculate average water system fees or rates from last 12 months of bills.
55. Or confirm well status, depth and output from Well Report.
56. Research/verify natural gas availability, supplier's name and phone number.
57. Verify security system, term of service and whether owned or leased.
58. Verify if seller has transferable Termite Bond.
59. Ascertain need for lead-based paint disclosure.
60. Prepare detailed list of property amenities and assess market impact.
61. Prepare detailed list of property's "Inclusions & Conveyances with Sale."
62. Complete list of completed repairs and maintenance items.
63. Send "Vacancy Checklist" to seller if property is vacant.
64. Explain benefits of Home Owner Warranty to seller.
65. Assist sellers with completion and submission of Home Owner Warranty application.
66. When received, place Home Owner Warranty in property file for conveyance at time of sale.
67. Have extra key made for lockbox.
68. Verify if property has rental units involved.
69. Make copies of all leases for retention in listing file.
70. Verify all rents and deposits.
71. Inform tenants of listing and discuss how showings will be handled.
72. Arrange for yard sign installation.
73. Assist seller with completion of Seller's Disclosure form.
74. Complete "new listing checklist."
75. Review results of Curb Appeal Assessment with seller and suggest improvements.
76. Review results of Interior Decor Assessment and suggest changes to shorten time on market.

77. Load listing time into transaction management software.

Entering Property in MLS Database

78. Prepare MLS Profile Sheet for accuracy of listing data.
79. Enter property data from Profile Sheet into MLS listing database.
80. Proofread MLS database listing for accuracy, including property placement in mapping function.
81. Add property to company's Active Listings.
82. Provide seller with signed copies of Listing Agreement and MLS Profile Data Form within 48 hours.
83. Take more photos for upload into MLS and use in flyers. Discuss efficacy of panoramic photography.

Marketing the Listing

84. Create print and Internet ads with seller's input.
85. Coordinate showings with owners, tenants and other agents. Return all calls–weekends included.
86. Install electronic lockbox. Program with agreed-upon showing time windows.
87. Prepare mailing and contact list.
88. Generate mail-merge letters to contact list.
89. Order "Just Listed" labels and reports.
90. Prepare flyers and feedback forms.
91. Review comparable MLS listings regularly to ensure property remains competitive in price, terms, conditions and availability.
92. Prepare property marketing brochure for seller's review.
93. Arrange for printing or copying of supply of marketing brochures or flyers.
94. Place marketing brochures in all company agent mailboxes.
95. Upload listing to company and agent Internet sites, if applicable.
96. Mail "Just Listed" notice to all neighborhood residents.
97. Advise Network Referral Program of listing.
98. Provide marketing data to buyers from international relocation networks.
99. Provide marketing data to buyers coming from referral network.

100. Provide "Special Feature" cards form marketing, if applicable
101. Submit ads to company's participating Internet real estate sites.
102. Convey price changes promptly to all Internet groups.
103. Reprint/supply brochures promptly as needed.
104. Review and update loan information in MLS as required.
105. Send feedback e-mails/faxes to buyers' agents after showings.
106. Review weekly Market Study.
107. Discuss feedback from showing agents with seller to determine if changes will accelerate the sale.
108. Place regular weekly update calls to seller to discuss marketing and pricing.
109. Promptly enter price changes in MLS listings database.

The Offer and the Contract

110. Receive and review all Offer to Purchase contracts submitted by buyers or buyers' agents.
111. Evaluate offer(s) and prepare "net sheet" on each for owner to compare.
112. Counsel seller on offers. Explain merits and weakness of each component of each offer.
113. Contact buyers' agents to review buyer's qualifications and discuss offer.
114. Fax/deliver Seller's Disclosure to buyer's agent or buyer upon request and prior to offer.
115. Confirm buyer is pre-qualified by calling loan officer.
116. Obtain pre-qualification letter on buyer from loan officer.
117. Negotiate all offers on seller's behalf, setting time limit for loan approval and closing date.
118. Prepare and convey any counteroffers, acceptance or amendments to buyer's agent.
119. Fax copies of contract and all addendums to closing attorney or title company.
120. When Offer-to-Purchase contract is accepted and signed by seller, deliver to buyer's agent.
121. Record and promptly deposit buyer's money into escrow account.
122. Disseminate "Under-Contract Showing Restrictions" as seller requests.
123. Deliver copies of fully signed Offer to Purchase contract to sellers.
124. Fax/deliver copies of Offer to Purchase contract to selling agent.
125. Fax copies of Offer to Purchase contract to lender.
126. Provide copies of signed Offer to Purchase contract for office file.
127. Advise seller in handling additional offers to purchase submitted between contract and closing.
128. Change MLS status to "Sale Pending."
129. Update transaction management program to show "Sale Pending."

130. Review buyer's credit report results–Advise seller of worst and best case scenarios.
131. Provide credit report information to seller if property is to be seller financed.
132. Assist buyer with obtaining financing and follow up as necessary.
133. Coordinate with lender on discount points being locked in with dates.
134. Deliver unrecorded property information to buyer.
135. Order septic inspection, if applicable.
136. Receive and review septic system report and access any impact on sale.
137. Deliver copy of septic system inspection report to lender and buyer.
138. Deliver well flow test report copies to lender, buyer and listing file.
139. Verify termite inspection ordered.
140. Verify mold inspection ordered, if required.

Tracking the Loan Process

141. Confirm return of verifications of deposit and buyer's employment.
142. Follow loan processing through to the underwriter.
143. Add lender and other vendors to transaction management program so agents, buyer and seller can track progress of sale.
144. Contact lender weekly to ensure processing is on track.
145. Relay final approval of buyer's loan application to seller.

Home Inspection

146. Coordinate buyer's professional home inspection with seller.
147. Review home inspector's report.
148. Enter completion into transaction management tracking software program.
149. Explain seller's responsibilities of loan limits and interpret any clauses in the contract.
150. Ensure seller's compliance with home inspection clause requirements.
151. Assist seller with identifying and negotiating with trustworthy contractors for required repairs.
152. Negotiate payment and oversee completion of all required repairs on seller's behalf, if needed.

The Appraisal

153. Schedule appraisal.
154. Provide comparable sales used in market pricing to appraiser.
155. Follow up on appraisal.
156. Enter completion into transaction management program.
157. Assist seller in questioning appraisal report if it seems too low.

Closing Preparations and Duties

158. Make sure contract is signed by all parties.
159. Coordinate closing process with buyer's agent and lender.
160. Update closing forms and files.
161. Ensure all parties have all forms and information needed to close the sale.
162. Select location for closing.
163. Confirm closing date and time and notify all parties.
164. Solve any title problems (boundary disputes, easements, etc.) or in obtaining death certificates.
165. Work with buyer's agent in scheduling and conducting buyer's final walkthrough prior to closing.
166. Research all tax, HOA, utility and other applicable proration's.
167. Request final closing figures from closing agent (attorney or Title Company).
168. Receive and carefully review closing figures to ensure accuracy.
169. Forward verified closing figures to buyer's agent.
170. Request copy of closing documents from closing agent.
171. Confirm the buyer and buyer's agent received title insurance commitment.
172. Provide "Home Owners Warranty" for availability at closing.
173. Review all closing documents carefully for errors.
174. Forward closing documents to absentee seller as requested.
175. Review documents with closing agent (attorney).
176. Provide earnest money deposit from escrow account to closing agent.
177. Coordinate closing with seller's next purchase, resolving timing issues.
178. Have a "no surprises" closing so that seller receives a net proceeds check at closing.
179. Refer sellers to one of the best agents at their destination, if applicable.

180. Change MLS status to Sold. Enter sale date, price, selling broker and agent's ID numbers.
181. Close out listing in transaction management program.

Follow Up After Closing

182. Answer questions about filing claims with Home Owner Warranty company.
183. Attempt to clarify and resolve any repair conflicts if buyer is dissatisfied.
184. Respond to any follow-up calls and provide any additional information required from office files.

WORKBOOK

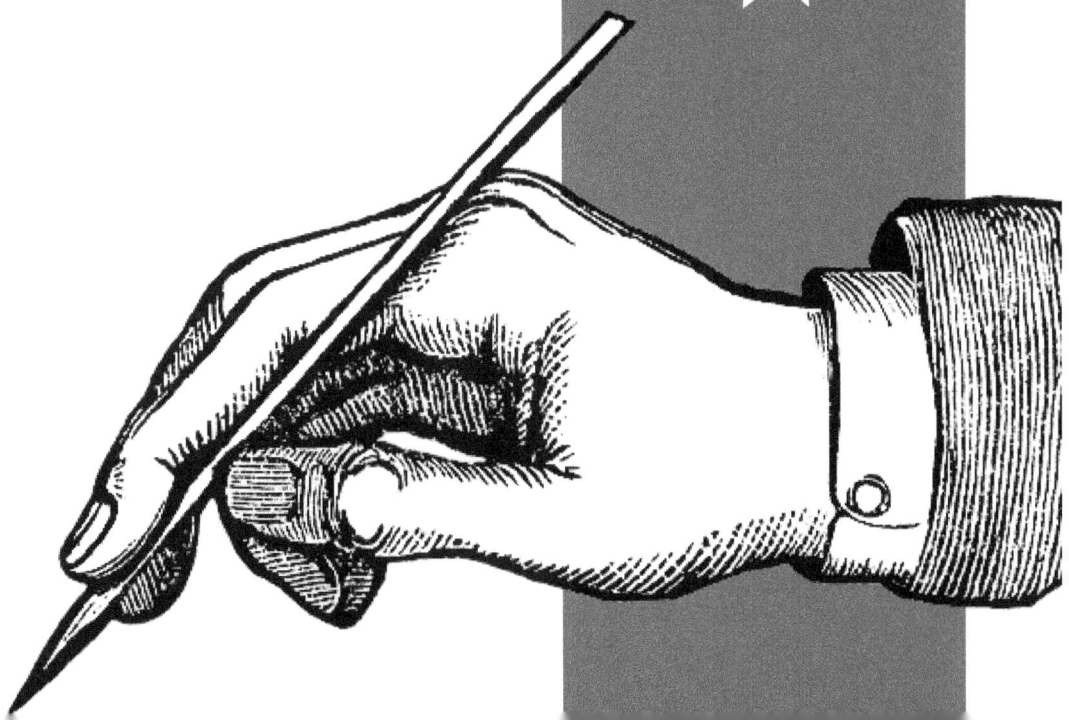

STEP 1

DECIDING WHAT YOU WANT

1. Single Story, 2 Story, Condo-, Co-op, Townhouse, Mobile Home, Multi family Duplex, Triplex, or Fourplex?
2. Where do you want to live? City?
3. How big do you want your house? Square footage?
4. New Construction or Existing Home?
5. Fixer upper or Move in Condition?
6. What style of home do you want? (Colonial, Farmhouse, Contemporary, Ranch, Victoria, Cape Cod)
7. Do you prefer Brick, Stone, Aluminum, Vinyl Siding or Stucco Exterior?
8. Do you want a bright house with a lot of windows or dark one?
9. Do you want a lot of land, a big back yard?
10. Do you want a deck, sundeck or patio?
11. What amenities to you want? (Pool, Jacuzzi, intercom etc.)
12. What type of parking? (Indoor, Outdoor, covered, attached, detached?)
13. How many bedrooms?
14. How many bathrooms?
15. Do you want a family room, game room, home office, den, library?
16. Do you want a fireplace? (Gas or wood burning)
17. Do you want an attic or basement?
18. Do you want your laundry area in the house or in the garage?
19. What type of closets do you want? How important is it to you 1-10?
20. What kind of appliances do you want?
21. What type of flooring do you want? (Hardwood, tile, carpet, marble)
22. How much money do you have for decorating after you move in?
23. Do you want central air and heating?
24. Do you want ceiling fans?

25. What kind of neighborhood you want to live in?
26. What school district do you prefer?
27. Do you want to live close to your kids school? How close?
28. How important is safety to you? Crime report?
29. Do you want a neighborhood that has a mixture of young & old people or the same age as you?
30. What percentage of children do you want in your neighborhood?
31. What kind of services do you want in your neighborhood? (Dry cleaners, stores, laundry mat, church etc.)
32. How do you plan to get to work? Is transportation nearby?
33. How far away do you want to live from your family and friends?

STEP #1

DECIDING WHAT YOU WANT

YOUR ANSWERS

1.____
2.____
3.____
4.____
5.____
6.____
7.____
8.____
9.____
10.____
11.____
12.____
13.____
14.____
15.____
16.____
17.____
18.____
19.____
20.____
21.____

22.____

23.____

24.____

25.____

26.____

27.____

28.____

29.____

30.____

31.____

32.____

33.____

STEP #1

ANSWERS

TOP 10 FROM YOUR LIST OF 33

1.____

2.____

3.____

4.____

5.____

6.____

7.____

8.____

9.____

10._______________________________________

TOP 5 FROM YOUR LIST OF 10

1.____

2.____

3.____

4.____

5.____

TOP 3 FROM YOUR LIST OF 5

1.____

2.____

3.____

MOST IMPORTANT OUT OF THE 3

1.____

Preliminary Questions

1. Know what is on your credit report? (Order a copy from 3 Bureaus)

2. What are your 3 fico scores? What is your middle fico score?

   i. Equifax Score________ Middle score_________
   ii. Trans Union Score________
   iii. Experian Score________

3. How much do you have to put down?
   i. 20%
   ii. 10% Deposit $__________
   iii. 5%
   iv. 3% or less ($5,000 earnest money)

4. What is the current going interest rate? _________

5. What can your afford monthly?
   Monthly mortgage payment you can afford? $ ____________
   What mortgage payment can you handle? $ ____________

6. What is the maximum amount of house you can afford? $ __________

a. Total purchase price of house $____________

7. Shopping for Lenders—Choose your lender

8. Choose your lender carefully. Look for financial stability and a reputation for customer satisfaction. Be sure to choose a company that gives helpful advice and that makes you feel comfortable. Ask your Realtor for recommendations. A good Realtor will have a working relationship with several lenders that they have had previous success with. Also ask friends and family for whom they have used. You will be surprised at their recommendations.

9. **Get a good faith estimate from the Lender.**

10. **Get a Prequalification letter from your Lender to give to your Realtor.**

Name of Lender____

Address of Lender______________________________________

Telephone #____________________ Fax #____________________

Name of Broker____

Notes____

STEP
3
CHOOSE A REALTOR

Reasons to use a Realtor

1. Trained and Held accountable by the Department of Real Estate
2. They are your eyes and ears in the marketplace.
3. Less Legwork for you.
4. They will guide you in the best direction. Saving you time and money.
5. They will educate you. Knowledge is power!
6. They will do all of your paperwork.
7. They will negotiate the very best deal for you!

How to find a Good Realtor

1. Word of Mouth
2. Neighborhood Advertisement
3. Realtor who has sold in your area
4. Internet

Things to ask your Realtor

1. Will you go out with me looking for homes? How often?
2. How do you find properties? Explain the process.
3. How long have you been a Realtor? How many transactions have you done?
4. What is your process for helping me find my home?
5. Are you a licensed Realtor?
6. How often will I get to talk to you?

7. Do I have direct access to you when I need you or will I talk to your assistant?
8. Do you have a website? A personal brochure?
9. Are you a full time Realtor or part time Realtor?

What are the 3 most important things you want from your Realtor:

1____

2____

3____

REALTOR CHOSEN

Name of Realtor ________________________________

Name of Realtors Real Estate Firm________________________

Address of Realtors office____________________________

Realtors Direct Phone #_____________________________

Realtors Office #____________________ Fax #________________

Notes____

STEP

4

LOCATE YOUR PROPERTY

Refer to Step #1—Give summary to your Realtor

1. Go out looking for property with your Realtor
2. If you go out on your own—Make sure that you tell the other Realtors that you are working with an Agent. **(Have their card handy to give to the other Realtors - Loyalty to your Realtor is crucial!)**
3. Compare the properties to your summary in ***Step #1***
4. Ask yourself:

   Is this property what I envisioned? Yes No

   Would I be happy living here? Yes No

   Does it feel like home? Yes No

   Does it meet my basic needs? Yes No

   Does my family like it? Yes No

   On a scale from 1-10—How does it rate?
   (1 lowest & 10 highest) ___________

5. Give the top 3 properties that you like to your Realtor
6. Don't get discouraged!

   Please know that looking for a home/property can be stressful, discouraging,disappointing and tiring! The process could take 1 day or it can takes weeks to months. Do not be too picky to the point that you dismiss every property that you see because it isn't perfect. Look for the top 3 things on your list, and ask yourself about the other things that you are not found of:

   Can I live with this? Yes No

   Will this kill me? Yes No

   Can I change this? Yes No

   Can I do with/without this? Yes No

7. When you find the property that you like—**Make your best offer fast!**

ADDRESSES OF PROPERTIES CHOSEN:

______________________	______________________
______________________	______________________
______________________	______________________
______________________	______________________

WHAT IS AN OFFER: An offer is a promise conditioned upon some requested or asked for promise. An offer demonstrates intent by one party to form a contract with another party.

FORMS NEEDED: *(not limited to this list)*

1—California Residential Purchase Agreement & Joint Escrow Instructions

2—Addendum to Purchase Agreement & Joint Escrow Instructions

3—Buyer's Inspection Advisory

4—Broker's Addendum

5—Disclosure Regarding Real Estate Agency Relationships

6—Disclosure and Consent for Representation of More than One Buyer or Seller

7—Wood Destroying Pest Inspection & Allocation of Cost Addendum

ITEMS NEEDED BY REALTOR WHEN OFFER IS SUBMITTED:

1—Deposit Check

2—Proof of Funds (A bank statement showing the deposit money is in the bank)

3—1st Page of Credit Report (showing fico scores)

4—Personal Letter to Seller *(Written by you or your Realtor)*

(Who you are and why the seller should sell you their home)

5—Pre Approval Letter (From your Lender)

6—Your Offer (California Residential Purchase Agreement & Joint Escrow Instructions)

Note: Although the sellers Real Estate Agent may not request all of these items, it makes your offer stronger if it gets to a multiple counter offer status.

Counter Offer

A counter offer are the conditions on which the Sellers Agent will accept the offer you presented. Some of the conditions that are to be changed could be: Price increase, loan or appraisal contingency removed, deposit to be increased, escrow, title, home warranty or other sellers services added or specified, Section 1 of Termite to be paid by Buyer, etc.

Review counter offer, negotiate then reject or accept offer.

If you accept the offer—Go to Step #6

STEP 6

WITHIN 3–7 DAYS AFTER ACCEPTANCE OF OFFER

1—By now you should be in **escrow with and escrow #.**

Your deposit check should be in escrow by now.

2—Start shopping for **Home Insurance** (Fire & Hazard)

3—Don't purchase any major things on your credit or apply for any new credit cards without talking to your lender. One negative movement on your credit could result in you losing your loan—thus losing your house.

4—Be accessible to your Realtor & Lender to sign documents, or provide any Requested paperwork. Please note that time is of the essence. You need to respond to any requests from Escrow, your Realtor or Lender as quickly as possible.

Escrow Company____

Address____

____

Phone#____________________

Escrow#_______________________________

Escrow Officer's Name____________________________________

Home Insurance
Company____

Address____

____

Phone #_________________________

Policy#__________________________

Contact Name____

STEP

7

WITHIN 7–17 DAYS

	Ordered	Completed
1—CONDUCT INSPECTIONS:		
Home Inspection	( )	( )
2—REVIEW DISCLOSURES AND SIGN:		
Transfer Disclosure Statement		( )
Supplemental Statutory Disclosure		( )
Lead Based Paint Addendum		( )
Smoke Detector Statement of Compliance		( )
Water Heater Statement of Compliance		( )
Defective Furnace Disclosure		( )
Toxic Mold Disclosure		
Residential Hazard & Earthquake Safety Booklet		( )
Preliminary Title Report		( )
Zone Disclosure Report		
Natural Hazard Disclosure Statement		( )
3—Make sure Your Lender has ordered the Appraisal	( )	( )
4—Review Reports:		
Home Inspection	Date Reviewed	( )
Termite Inspection and/or Clearance	Date Reviewed	( )

5—Request for Repairs

Have your Realtor go over Home Inspection Report and request for repairs for any items you want fixed, removed or addressed.

Date Requested ( ) Date Completed ( )

17th Day –Remove Contingencies or Cancel Contract

Date Contingency Removed ( ) or Date Contract Cancelled ( )

STEP 8

VERIFY PROGRESS WITH LENDER

Questions to ask your Lender:

1—Are there any conditions that I need to meet?

Conditions: ______________________________

____

____

2—Where are we in the loan process? ______________

3—Do I need to provide you with any more documents? Yes No

If yes—What items: ______________________________

____

____

____

4—When will my loan documents be ready to sign? Date ________

5—What will my mortgage payments be? Payment $____________

6—What is my interest rate?

On the first? %__________

On the Second loan? %__________

7—What type of loan do I have?

Interest only? 15 or 30 year fixed? Adjustable? 80/20 etc. ______

8—Are we on time for closing on time? Yes No

9—Estimated close date? Date______________

10—Did you get the appraisal back? Yes No

Did the value come in? Yes No

Things Lender will need:

1—W2's from past 2 years

2—Taxes from past 2 years

3—Copies of 1 month pay stubs

4—Copies of most recent bank statements

5—Copies of Divorce decree

6—List of last 7 addresses

Note: Don't be afraid to talk to your Lender! He is doing what is best for you. Make sure you let him know what your concerns and desires are!

STEP

9

VERIFICATION OF PROPERTY CONDITION

5 DAYS BEFORE THE CLOSE OF ESCROW

1. Do a final walk through of your property to make sure that the items you wanted fixed on your Request for Repairs are done, and to make sure that there is nothing odd or missing that was included in your Transfer Disclosure Statement. For example: pool didn't go green from neglect, big holes in the walls that wasn't there before, cabinets or light fixtures removed. Be sure to verify items that you requested to be fixed were indeed fixed.

   Note: This is also a time to have the sellers show you how things work around the house. For example: the heater, air conditioner, pool, lighting, garage doors, alarms, appliance hook ups, etc.

2. Sign the Verification of Property Condition

Things To Bring To Escrow When Signing Documents

1. Brings 2 forms of Picture ID
2. Cashier's check for balance of closing costs or deposit
3. Bring everyone who is on the Purchase Agreement

   (Everyone who needs to sign needs to be present)
4. Proof of Home Insurance

Things To Note When Signing Documents

1. Verify HUD #1—Estimated closing costs prepared by Escrow
2. Get copies of everything you need to sign
3. Don't sign anything unless you agree & understand it
4. Verify interest rates & monthly mortgage payments
5. Decide how you want to hold title on your home
6. If you want to add someone to your title—tell escrow to provide a Quick claim for you to sign with that person's name on it
7. Pay balance of closing costs and/or deposit.

STEP 11

WHAT ARE CLOSING COSTS?

List of closing costs

1. Lenders points, loan origination or loan service fee 0—3% of loan amount
2. Loan Application Fee $0-$500
3. Lenders Credit Report $20-$150
4. Lenders Processing Fee $75-$150
5. Lenders Documentation Fee $50-$200
6. Appraisal $200-$500
7. Prepaid Interest on the Loan (Daily cost of your loan from the Day of closing through the end of the month
8. Home Owners Insurance
9. First Premium or Mortgage Insurance (if applicable)
10. Property Tax (To cover tax period to date)
11. Escrow Service Fee
12. Title Company & Escrow closing $150-$1000
13. Recording Fee
14. Local City, County, Town, State Transfer Tax
15. Condo Move-In Fee

What do I get at closing?

1. Settlement Statement (HUD #1)
2. Truth in Lending Statement
3. Mortgage Note
4. Mortgage or Deed of Trust
5. Binding Sales Contract
6. Home Warranty Information
7. Termite Completion or Clearance
8. Keys to your Home

STEP

12

FUNDING

When a loan is approved, the Lender issues a commitment to make the loan at certain specific terms. When your deal is funded, monies are transferred to all parties involved. It is an act of supplying cash for the loan to all parties involved.

STEP

13

RECORDING

Recording occurs either the day the property is funded or 24 hours afterward. It is an act of entering in a book of public records instruments affecting the title to your property.

Recording in this manner gives notice to the world of the facts recorded.

For example: Who is the new owner of the property, how much the property was sold for, square footage of the property, how many bedrooms, baths etc.

By recording the deed from the sale of the property, the purchasers assumes that all subsequent interested parties are given notice of the purchaser's interests in the property.

THE HOUSE IS OFFICIALLY YOURS!

STEP 14

MOVING

EIGHTH WEEK CHECKLIST

General Information

Name of Person Moving ______________________

Current Address ______________________

City, State, Zip ______________________

New Address ______________________

City, State, Zip ______________________

Moving Day ______________________

Moving Distance ______________________

Travel Time ______________________

The following should be completed **eight weeks** prior to moving day:

________ Draw a floor plan of your new home—decide what furniture will go where

________ Begin using up food in your freezer

________ Contact the **Chamber of Commerce** in your new area to get information on your new area

Adddress ______________________

Phone # ______________________

_____ Decide whether to use a professional mover or move yourself

_____ I will be moving myself

Use the following guide to determine the size of truck to rent

2 rooms or less—Cargo Van

2—3 rooms - 15 foot truck

3—6 rooms - 18 foot truck

7—8 rooms - 22 foot truck

_____ I will be using the following moving company:

Company Name________________________________

Contact Person________________________________

Address________________________________

City, State, Zip________________________________

Phone #____________________ Fax #____________________

_____ Company will provide:

_____Pre-planning _____Unpacking _____Packing

_____Packing boxes _____Packing crates _____Packing blankets

_____Packing labels _____Disposal of packing containers

_____Dollies _____Storage _____Damage Coverage

SIXTH WEEK CHECKLIST

The following should be completed **six weeks** prior to moving day:

_____ Gather records from your doctors, dentists, lawyers, accountant etc & place in safe place

_____ Make arrangement to transfer your children's school records

_____ Sell, transfer, refund, or resign all club or association memberships

_____ Contact your tax person about deductible moving expenses. Save all receipts!

_____ Go to the post office & get a change of address kit. Begin filling out the cards.

_____ Notify the following people:

___Relatives ___Accountant ___IRS ___Newspapers ___Banks

___Doctor ___Dentist ___Clubs ___Friends ___Lawyer

___Broker ___Creditors ___Magazines ___Auto Insurance ___Catalogs

___Tax Man ___Fire Insurance ___Health Insurance ___Life Insurance

___Homeowner's Insurance ___Credit Card Company

FOURTH WEEK CHECKLIST

The following should be completed **four weeks** prior to moving:

_____ Make arrangements to store any items

_____ Clean or repair any furniture, carpets, curtains that need it

_____ Hold a garage sale

_____ Return and retrieve borrowed items

_____ If you are moving yourself find out how many boxes you will need & where to purchase them

_____ Contact the moving company or rental company to confirm previous moving arrangements

THIRD WEEK CHECKLIST

The following items should be completed **three weeks** prior to moving:

_____ Begin packing items that you won't need.

_____ Contact a service technician to prepare your appliances for moving

_____ Have a going away party

_____ Decide what to do with house plants

_____ Make travel or hotel reservations if needed

_____ Arrange for pet travel if needed

_____ Properly service any automobile, boat, or trailer that will be moved or shipped

_____ Get automobile license, registration, and insurance in order

_____ Write on the packing boxes in what room the items belong

_____ Use a notebook for listing cartons as they are packed

Gather Packing Materials:

___	Furniture Pads	___	Dolly	___	Packing Tape
___	Styrofoam "peanuts"	___	Bubble Wrap	___	White or tissue Paper
___	Scissors	___	Labels & Stickers	___	Boxes
___	Gummed Tape	___	String & Rope	___	Garage Bags
___	Crumbled Newspaper	___	Utility knife	___	Crates

Cancel Basic Services To Your Old Home:

Electric:

Company Name: ____________________

Contact Person: ____________________

Phone Number: ____________________

Date Called: ____________________

Date Discontinued: ____________________

Gas/Oil:

Company Name: ______________________

Contact Person: ______________________

Phone Number: ______________________

Date Called: ______________________

Date Discontinued: ______________________

Water/Sewage/Garbage:

Company Name: ______________________

Contact Person: ______________________

Phone Number: ______________________

Date Called: ______________________

Date Discontinued: ______________________

Cable TV:

Company Name: ______________________

Contact Person: ______________________

Phone Number: ______________________

Date Called: ______________________

Date Discontinued: ______________________

Telephone:

Company Name: ______________________

Contact Person: ______________________

Phone Number: ______________________

Date Called: ______________________

Date Discontinued: ______________________

SECOND WEEK CHECKLIST

The following should be completed **two weeks** prior to moving day:

_____ Arrange to transfer all bank accounts and safety deposit box contents to new branch of bank

_____ Arrange for traveler's check to use for travel and first few days at your new home

_____ Cancel any direct deposit or automatic payment arrangements with the bank

_____ Begin serious packing of items you will not need over the next two weeks

_____ Send change of address cards and contact Post Office with forwarding address

_____ Service your automobile, especially if you are traveling a distance.

_____ Cancel delivery services, such as water deliveries or diaper services

SET UP BASIC SERVICES TO YOUR NEW HOME

Electric:

Company Name: ______________________________

Contact Person: ______________________________

Phone Number: ______________________________

Date Called: ______________________________

Date Service Begins: ______________________________

Gas/Oil:

Company Name: ______________________________

Contact Person: ______________________________

Phone Number: ______________________________

Date Called: ______________________________

Date Service Begins: ______________________________

Water/Sewage/Garbage:

Company Name: ______________________________

Contact Person: ______________________________

Phone Number: ______________________________

Date Called: ______________________________

Date Service Begins: ______________________________

Cable TV:

Company Name: ______________________________

Contact Person: ______________________________

Phone Number: ______________________________

Date Called: ______________________________

Date Service Begins: ______________________________

Telephone:

Company Name: ______________________________

Contact Person: ______________________________

Phone Number: ______________________________

Date Called: ______________________________

Date Service Begins: ______________________________

FIRST WEEK CHECKLIST

The following should be completed **one week** prior to moving day:

_____ Get measurements of your new home's doors and hallways. Make note of stairs and entryways.

_____ Transfer all medical prescriptions to a pharmacy in your new location

_____ Return library books and videotapes

_____ Pick up any dry cleaning, layaway, or any stored items

THREE DAY CHECKLIST

The following should be completed **three days prior** to moving day:

_____ Defrost and clean your refrigerator and freezer

_____ Movers begin packing

_____ Pack suitcases for your trip to your new home

_____ Arrange to have payment ready to pay the driver or rental company.

_____ Remember to pack the attic, closets, cabinets, and other storage areas

_____ Be sure to empty water for your steam iron

_____ Launder all soiled clothing

_____ Take your old phone book with you

_____ Set aside valuables and legal documents that will go with you, not in the moving van

Pack your "Moving Day" handy items box:

___	First Aid Kit	___	Paper towels	___	Disposable dishes
___	Bath towels	___	Light bulbs	___	Trash bags
___	Shelf liner	___	Sponge	___	Camera/film/batteries

___ Dish Detergent
___ Daily medicine
___ Dish towels
___ Plastic utensils
___ Toiletries
___ Tools
___ Telephone Book
___ Snacks
___ Soap
___ Road Map
___ Water
___ Bathroom Tissue

MOVING DAY CHECKLIST

The following should be completed on **moving day**:

_____ Pick up moving truck early if you are moving yourself

_____ List every item and box loaded onto the truck

_____ Tell the mover where you can be reached. Leave a phone number.

_____ Keep the moving company bill or rental receipt in a safe place until everything is done

Remember to check your old home for the following:

___ Turn off water
___ Turn off air conditioning
___ Inspect cabinets
___ Turn of lights
___ Turn off appliances
___ Lock all windows
___ Lock all doors
___ Leave garage door opener
___ Surrender old house keys
___ Inspect rooms
___ Inspect closets
___ Inspect garage

DELIVERY CHECKLIST

The following should be completed on **delivery day**:

_____ Advise your mover of any parking restrictions, elevators or long carries

_____ Make certain the house is ready for occupancy, before the mover arrives

_____ Place a floor plan of your new home at the front door

_____ Be on hand to answer questions, give directions, and examine your items

_____ Check off all boxes and items as they come off the truck

_____ Install new locks in your new home

_____ Test to make sure the utilities are hooked up

_____ Test smoke detectors

_____ Set up beds early

_____ Pay moving or rental company

_____ Unpack kids toys early

_____ Apply shelf lining in the kitchen

_____ Return the moving rental truck, if one was used

AFTER DELIVERY CHECKLIST

_____ Get acquainted with your new town. Locate the school, grocery store and other businesses

_____ Register to vote

_____ Ask neighbors, and friends for doctors, dentist, accountant, lawyer, bank, baby sitter, etc.

_____ Transfer current medical information to new professionals

_____ Locate the hospital as well as police and fire stations near you

_____ Plan and practice your fire escape route

_____ Visit the library and apply for a card

_____ Have a service technician perform post-moving service to your appliances

_____ Mail that has been forwarded from your old address will need a change of address car sent

_____ Keep documents pertaining to your move in a safe place. Be sure to keep all receipts

_____ Get acquainted with the neighbors

_____ Have a house warming party

HOME BUYING ACTIVITY CHECKLIST

PRE—CONTRACT

( ) Locate a REALTOR

( ) Sign a buyer broker agreement with your Realtor

( ) Choose a Lender

( ) Locate your property

( ) Make an offer on the property

ACCEPTANCE

( ) Sign offer

( ) Sign Counter Offers (*If applicable)*

AFTER ACCEPTANCE

3 Days	( )	Give deposit to Escrow
3 Days	( )	Start shopping for Home Insurance (Fire & Hazard)
7 Days	( )	Give pre-qualification or pre-approval letter
7 Days	( )	Verify down payment & closing costs
7 Days	( )	Make sure Lender orders appraisal
7-17 Days	( )	Conduct inspections
7-17 Days	( )	Review reports
7-17 Days	( )	Request repairs
17 Days	( )	In writing, remove contingencies or cancel

17 Days	( )	Check status of your loan with the Lender
1-5 Days after Delivery	( )	Review HOA disclosures
5 Days after Delivery	( )	In writing, remove contingency for common interest disclosures or cancel
5 Days before close of escrow	( )	Verify Condition of property *(final walk through)*
Close of Escrow	( )	Sign loan documents
	( )	Property Funded
	( )	Property Recorded
Moving Day	( )	Move into your New Home!

YOUR TEAM

Realtor____Phone#_______________________

Broker____Phone#_______________________

Lender____Phone#_______________________

Home Inspection ________________________________Phone#_______________________

Home Warranty_________________________________Phone#_______________________

Home Insurance_________________________________Phone#_______________________

Other:____Phone#_______________________

Other:____Phone#______________________

Other:____Phone#______________________

Other:____Phone#______________________

Other:____Phone#______________________

JOURNAL

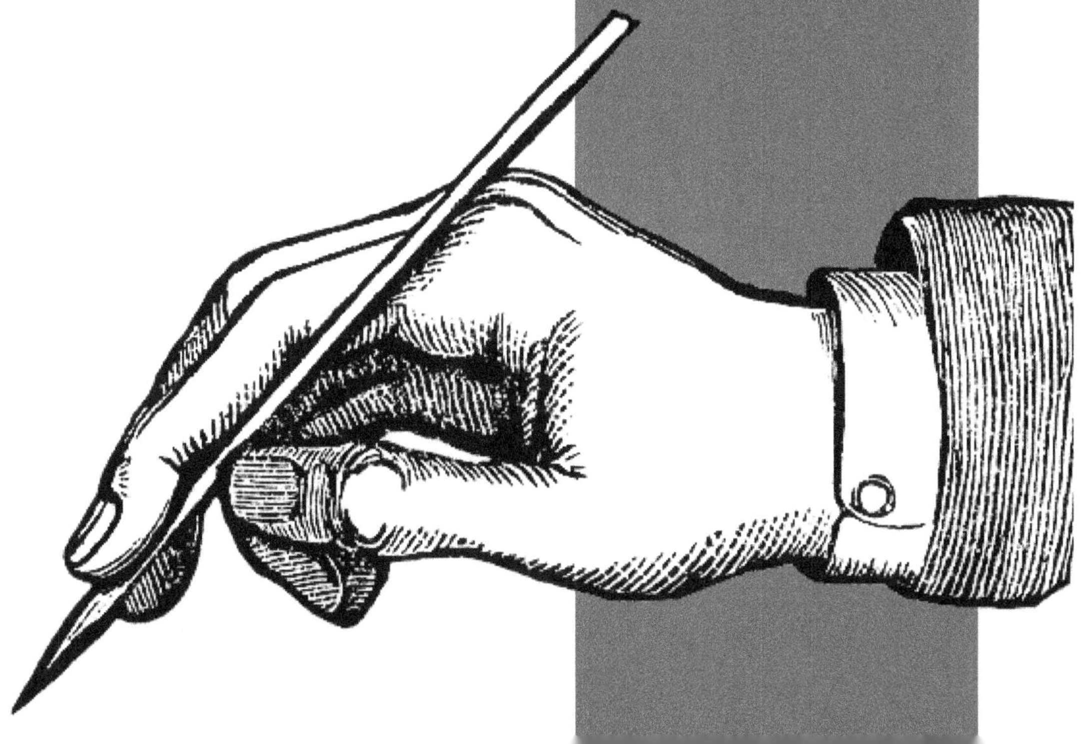

YOUR JOURNEY JOURNAL

Journaling is a vehicle of emotional exploration, a way to channel difficult feelings into healthy and creative outcomes. By writing down your thoughts and feelings, you can focus on what you are feeling and paying attention to everything that is going on. You will be forced to confront your feelings rather than run away from them.

Reflective writing has also been shown to improve decision making and critical thinking. Writing clarifies thinking.

Recording your thoughts in a medium outside your own head clears out that storage. As a result, your mind becomes quieter. You can begin to think more clearly.

Make sure that you write in the journal when something monumental happens or you feel anxiety, confusion or something noteworthy of writing about. The more consistent you can keep your journaling routine, the beneficial it will be to you.

Jot down those moments of inspiration or nagging thoughts that you have as soon as you can; this will help get them out of your head so you can focus on the bigger picture of securing your dream home and not on the small unimportant things.

You can challenge yourself to write about one thing every day during the transaction—something you are grateful for or something that you will always remember.

In this section- simply **write** down your thoughts and feelings to understand them much more clearly during each phase of this process.

Happy Exploration—Be honest and pay attention to your thoughts.

Date: ____________________

Thoughts: ____

____

____

____

____

____

____

____

____

____

____

____

Date: ____________________

Thoughts: ____

Date: ____________________

Thoughts: ____

Date: ____________________

Thoughts: ____

Date: ____________________

Thoughts: ____________________

Date: ____________________

Thoughts: ____________________

Date: ____________________

Thoughts: ____________________

Date: ____________________

Thoughts: ____________________

Date: ____________________

Thoughts: ____________________

Date: ____________________

Thoughts: ____________________

Date: ____________________

Thoughts: ____

Date: ____________________

Thoughts: ____

Date: ____________________

Thoughts: ____

Date: ____________________

Thoughts: ____________________

Date: ____________________

Thoughts: ____________________

Date: ____________________

Thoughts: ____________________

Date: ____________________

Thoughts: ____________________

Date: ____________________

Thoughts: ____________________

Date: ____________________

Thoughts: ____________________

Date: ____________________

Thoughts: ____________________

Date: ____________________

Thoughts: ____________________

Date: ____________________

Thoughts: ____________________

Date: ____________________

Thoughts: ____________________

Date: ____________________

Thoughts: ____________________

Date: ____________________

Thoughts: ____________________

Date: ____________________

Thoughts: ____

Date: ____________________

Thoughts: ____

Date: ____________________

Thoughts: ____

Date: ____________________

Thoughts: ____

Date: ____________________

Thoughts: ____

Date: ____________________

Thoughts: ____

Date: ____________________

Thoughts: ____________________

Date: ____________________

Thoughts: ____________________

Date: ____________________

Thoughts: ____________________

Date: ____________________

Thoughts: ____________________

Date: ____________________

Thoughts: ____________________

Date: ____________________

Thoughts: ____________________

Date: ____________________

Thoughts: ____________________

Date: ____________________

Thoughts: ____________________

Date: ____________________

Thoughts: ____________________

Date Moved In_________

My Dream House!

Date Bought ___________________

Price $_______________________

What I like the most about my new home ____

What I remember most during the process ____

Who I appreciate the most ____

Who helped me the most ____

What I learned about myself during the process ____

What would I have done differently ____

What would I say to someone buying a house for the 1st time ____

What I am most grateful for about my new house ____

Address ____

City __________________________ State ______________ Zip_____________

CONGRATULATIONS!

YOU HAVE MADE IT! NOW ENJOY YOUR NEW HOME!!

www.ingramcontent.com/pod-product-compliance
Lightning Source LLC
Chambersburg PA
CBHW081536220326
41598CB00036B/6452